Open H✝S Word

Emily Zondlak

Chapbook Press

Schuler Books
2660 28th Street SE
Grand Rapids, MI 49512
(616) 942-7330
www.schulerbooks.com

Open His Word

ISBN 13: 9781943359349

eBook ISBN: 9781948237598

Library of Congress Control Number: 2016939815 (Paperback edition)

Copyright © 2020 Emily Zondlak

All rights reserved. No part of this book may be reproduced in any form except for the purpose of brief reviews, without written permission of the author.

Printed in the United States by Chapbook Press.

Open H†S Word

Introduction

Sometimes we do not understand God's Word (the Bible) and are afraid to ask for help. There is so much packed in the Word that it can be overwhelming. From one person to another it can be interpreted differently, but God's Word never returns void. God continues to change lives and build intimate relationships with His children!

What God has blessed me with is the gift of writing encouragements that glorify Him. I humbly and confidently stand before the throne of God to acknowledge that He has chosen me to write this book. I give Him all of the glory, honor, and praise!

God has allowed me to outline His Word by writing encouragements that are positive and challenging. I pray that this will deepen your relationship with God Almighty and your understanding. Jesus loves you!

Open H†S Word

Genesis

Chapters 1-7 God will provide for our every need. We have to trust and obey Him.

Chapters 1-7 God creates everything and has a plan. Choices will bring blessings or consequences. Remember God creates a way to have a relationship with Him. Trust and lean fully on God because people can be unreliable. Life plans are different so follow God's lead.

Chapters 7-14 In the world people are tempted to do and say things in the heat of the moment. Some people have an attitude of helping others out to receive the glory. Just remember to give the glory to God. Some things won't work as you planned so you run away from it. When God tells you to go back and face it, do it because it will benefit you!

Chapters 7-14 Lot's wife became a pillar of salt because she looked back when instructed not to. This can be a lesson of obeying and trusting God. Look forward to keep moving forward on the journey that God has planned. God has everything lined up. Just follow God's lead!

Open H†S Word

Chapters 7-14 Many people think about the negative outcomes in life. Stop doing that because it makes the situation worse. The end result may surprise you and be a blessing to you!

Chapters 14-21 Lessons are learned in life, but it is in the trials that make people stronger. Short cuts may spring up, but journeying through the long paths will make a person a better person. Some things should be kept secret because God wants to work on you. God will reveal it if or when He is ready to glorify Himself and to bless you. Patience is the key!

Chapters 21-28 People often think that some tasks are pointless in life. God knows where you are at and what you need. Keep doing what you know that God wants you to do and He will bless you! Jumping through hoops and tearing down strongholds may be required. Keep your eyes on God and victory is yours! Waiting on and trusting God can be hard, but it's rewarding!

End of <u>Genesis</u>

Exodus

Chapters 1-7 When someone plans for something to be bad, God can turn it around to bring blessings. Do not doubt yourself because God will speak through you to get His purpose completed! With Him, anything is possible!

Chapters 7-14 Followers of Jesus Christ, be bold to stand up to people when God tells you to. Don't give up trying because God's breakthrough will come! "But I have raised you up for this very purpose, that I might show you My power and that My Name might be proclaimed in all the earth." (Exodus 9:16 NIV) And Moses said to the people, "Fear not, stand firm, and see the salvation of the LORD, which he will work for you today. For the Egyptians whom you see today, you shall never see again. The LORD will fight for you, and you have only to be silent." (Exodus 14:13-14 ESV)

Chapters 15-21 Sometimes people develop an idea and they want to form it into a reality. So the process starts, but their loved ones are seeing that the person is wearing out. Receiving help is hard but it helps make things smoother! In the circumstances of life God

Open H✝S Word

may test you for what your obedience and trust levels for Him are. So remember to do God's will always!

Chapters 22-29 Projects can be rewarding especially when you are communicating with God during it. Once a person is finished, the peacefulness may disappear because an activity may be happening that wasn't planned. So emotions take control and it seems like everything outside is ruined. Relax! God will help you work everything out if your heart belongs to Him!

End of <u>Exodus</u>

Open H✝S Word

Leviticus

Chapters 1-7 In the beginning of followers' of Christ journeys, everybody is on fire for the Lord. We want to grow in the Lord and tell everyone about Him to grow God's kingdom. Years pass by and the zeal for God isn't what it used to be. Trials come and go that test your relationship with God. Do not lose your saltiness! Keep seeking God because He is molding you!

"For the life of a creature is in the blood." (Leviticus 17:11) Jesus shed blood for His children to have and enjoy life. So why not follow and trust Him through life?

Chapters 8-21 Many people take on more than enough. Stop! Bless others because it will be rewarding.

Chapters 22-27 Satan often makes what is good look bad and makes the bad look good. Step back to think about if the situation pleases God or upsets Him. If it upsets Him, don't worry, He will tell you in His own special way. The fear of God needs to come back and be taken seriously. God can and will do anything to benefit you. So why not trust and follow Him?

End of <u>Leviticus</u>

Open H†S Word

Numbers

Chapters 1-7 Everything and everyone has a purpose. God works through circumstances and His children to make a great plan!

Chapters 1-7 Can you hear God's voice? Often His children get wrapped up in circumstances that they do not seek God's will. Pay attention to His voice because following Him is incredible! Build a strong and intimate relationship with God! Stop letting your outside forces control you.

Chapters 8-21 It's so humbling to hear God's children asking for prayer or waiting on Him in prayer. God blesses His children with specific gifts. Many people compare themselves to others. Stop because God has created you for a specific purpose. God will reveal it when He knows you are mature to handle it. Keep your eyes on Him and everything will work out!

Chapters 22-28 It is easy to complain during trials because the end result may not be near in sight. Often people want to turn back instead of proceeding to the finish line. Don't let your emotions control you. Press on and move forward because God's plan is worth experiencing!

Open H✝S Word

Chapters 29-36 People's intensions can be good or bad. Sometimes God gives us wake-up calls to focus or re-focus our attention back to Him. Don't ignore problems because it may be God speaking to you to help you avoid a painful road.

End of <u>Numbers</u>

Open H†S Word

Deuteronomy

Chapters 1-7 Sometimes people accept bribes to ease the pressure of doing something that they don't want to do. Ask yourself "Does Jesus do that?" The answer is "No." Try to be fair. Show love and kindness. Don't think that you're better than everybody else because you're not! God doesn't judge by status and neither should we. What is in the heart is what matters!

Chapters 8-34 Laws are set up for guidance. Following God's commands is the best because you are being obedient and spreading God's love around! God may bless you by promoting you for better experiences.

End of Deuteronomy

Open H†S Word

Joshua

Chapters 1-7 Experiences mold you. Be bold, courageous, and do not stop following God's commands. People want instant blessings, but they may stumble off of God's straight and narrow path for their lives because they are not patient. God won't forget to bless His children because everything is in God's perfect timing.

Chapters 8-24 When a person realizes that he or she lives in a small world, the feelings can be mixed. People should be striving forward and helping others turn toward God by showing love and kindness.

End of Joshua

Open H†S Word

Judges

Chapters 1-7 I remember when I put my trust in others to grow my faith instead of seeking God. This is good when you are a new believer but the training wheels have to come off some time. Seek God because He wants to take care of you! God may ask you to do something to benefit you and to glorify Him. Answers may come for encouragement.

Chapters 8-21 I remember when I did and said things at the heat of the moment. If you are that kind of person, I hope that you realize that you are digging yourself in a pit. God will and wants to take care of you when you realize that He is the Power Source. Fall in love with God because He can do far above our understanding if our hearts are right!

End of Judges

Open H✝S Word

Ruth

Chapters 1-4 Sometimes people think that life is hopeless. Some things will not work out as you planned. Don't give up on doing what you know is right. Attitudes and being respectful will make or break trials. God's blessings are incredible to receive if you follow His plan for your life.

Chapters 1-4 Actions tell what is in the heart. Words ruin relationships, but if you seek God wholeheartedly and wait patiently, He will turn circumstances around. Don't stop acting Christ-like when trials arise because God and people are watching! Seek God because His plan works and is beyond comprehension!

End of Ruth

Open H†S Word

1 Samuel

Chapters 1-7 Often people do not understand the actions that others complete. Sometimes some actions are better unexplained so that God's plan can work and for Him to be glorified. Don't miss an opportunity to speak boldly when God speaks a word to you to say to others. It may be encouraging; answers to a prayer or a reminder to not to travel down that road. Seek God because He will take care of you. If you don't, you are creating problems and provoking Him to anger.

Chapters 8-14 People pray for things that they think would be satisfying. God may give people their requests to teach them a lesson about patience and relying on Him. Quit behaving as the world behaves, such as accepting bribes because you know better than that. Speak boldly to correct others.

Chapters 15-21 God uses the unlikely people to lead His people. The leader can be wholly for many years and follow God. Then the leader gets comfortable in which, he or she leans less on God and acts out of peer pressure. Don't get too comfortable in situations because things of this world are changing. Remain trusting and following God on the mountains AND valleys.

Chapters 22-28 When you are in a trial or have angry feelings toward another person, it is helpful to have good friends who encourage you and steer your focus back on God. Trials are when your relationship with God gets stronger and deeper. In the trial, you may become tempted to do evil. You can choose to do what's right and the end result will turn into something positive.

Chapters 29-31 Many times in life people think that they have life "all together" or "figured out." Some will not listen to others' advise because they are too full of themselves. When the wiser person is gone and when things are spinning out of control, the self-centered person will wish that he or she had listened. So be willing to learn from others. Remember God can repay evil for good if hearts are right.

Chapters 30-31 Often there are circumstances where things don't make sense. Things were going smoothly, but then a change happens. Will you listen to peer pressure, be upset, or do God's

Open H†S Word

will? Seek God and He will glorify Himself and bless you abundantly!

End of <u>1 Samuel</u>

Open H†S Word

2 Samuel

Chapters 1-7 People need to think before they act. An act can feel good for a moment, but the consequences can be deadly. People need to stop looking for approval from others and be concerned with what God thinks. Sometimes people backslide on their journey with God. Consequences are bound to show up so remember to include God in everything as if it were the beginning stage in your relationship.

Chapters 8-14 In life, there are evil schemes that come up. People stab others in the back or only look out for themselves. If people get others involved, there will be many damaged relationships. Destruction may be the result so the choice whether or not to follow God can be made.

Chapters 15-24 Mistakes may have to be taken care of at a later time. The repayment made be rewarding if hearts of right.

Chapters 22-24 Remember your trials and how God rescued you. Circumstances will not make sense, but seek, trust and obey Christ! Continue to do what pleases God! Praise and worship the Lord!   End of 2 Samuel

Open H†S Word

1 Kings

Chapters 1-7 Some people think that they are the best so they exalt themselves as a leader. The "leader" may seek and receive support from others. When this news gets to the authorities, control will be taken back to set things straight. The exalted will become humbled and the humbled will become exalted. God can and will do incredible actions by what our hearts say!

Chapters 8-14 We are in the habit of associating people by their past or who their family members are. Perceptions can change when people get to know each other or a mature action surfaces. God can use anyone to expand His kingdom, but having a humble attitude and a wiliness to endure trials are the keys. Try standing out of the crowd with God's help because wisdom can be planted.

Chapters 9-14 When you're told what to do for years, you may or may not always listen. God will get His point across. It's easy to do things yourself, but the Father has the ultimate control! Don't compare yourself to others or follow their lead. Open your heart to Christ and be honest. His plan is far better than yours!

Open H✝S Word

Chapters 15-21 Many people do not understand how to live the way that God wants them to live. If God's children are not living by example, it's so hard for people to know God and know what is from Satan. Dig deep in finding out who God is, know His promises, and seek guidance from other followers of Christ. He will begin to mold you!

Chapters 21-22 Often people want something that they can't have. They will complain, be somber, and look to others for help. If God the Father doesn't bless people with the desire, they won't be satisfied once they receive it. Christ will bless people if their hearts and motives are right! Be Christ's salt and light in this world! Stop conforming to this world and start transforming it for Christ!

Chapter 22 Often people complain about problems or loved ones for different reasons. Some people will ask for others' property and may not receive it. So the wanting people will have others involved and the property may be handed over. How a person received it may not be satisfying. In other instances, seeking advise from others can be touchy because people can be

Open H†S Word

encouraged or discouraged by it. The adviser should tell the truth no matter what.

End of <u>1 Kings</u>

2 Kings

Chapters 1-7 Trials come in seasons. Sometimes going through trials is positive because it can make your relationship with God stronger. I have learned that too much help can make the trial worse. On the other hand, you may need guidance from others. With everything, pray because God has the answers that you need.

Chapters 1-7 History can be interesting and is made everyday. Live how you want to be remembered. Actions have positive and negative outcomes. If you take a step back and don't like what you see, ask God to help you change. If you like what you see, continue on your journey.

Chapters 8-14 What is in a person's heart is displayed through actions. It's easy to follow by example from peers, in which you are associated with. God knows a person's heart because He knows everything. Nothing can be kept a secret from Him. He will care for you and work things out if you seek Him wholeheartedly. You can be a light in this darken world. Traditions may need to be broken to seek God and start a relationship with Him.

Open H†S Word

Chapters 8-14 It's easy to follow the crowd or cheat at things. If you're disobedient, you'll reap the consequences. If you know what the Lord wants, He'll work everything out for good! There comes a time when you have to decide if you're following Christ no matter what or if you're going to buckle to this world. You reap what you sow and silence may be needed to seek Christ!

Chapters 15-25 People have different gifts and abilities that God blesses them with. It's easy to complain, compare and be jealous of other people's gifts.

Chapters 22-25 You have a choice. When you accept Christ as your Lord and Savior, with the Holy Spirit's guidance, you can change the world and set it on fire for Christ. The other option is to conform to this world and go through the motions. Be bold and courageous! Stand up and be firm for Christ, allowing Him to orchestrate His plan!

End of 2 Kings

Open H†S Word

1 Chronicles

Chapters 1-7 Some people enjoy figuring out the genealogy of their family. Property may be handed down for many reasons. On the other hand, some people do not care to know the genealogy because they may feel as if it is a waste of time. Sometimes it is neat to look at each family member because each family member is journeying on different pathways. God constructs different plans.

Chapters 8-14 It is often difficult to come up with words how grateful you are to God when He has blessed you with so much! Once you start praising Him, no matter if it's in the highest moments or the lowest moments, you will have a difficult time stopping! Satan is sneaky and will try to make you do things that will be tempting. Pray about everything because God will guide you!

Chapters 15-29 The body of Christ has many parts working together in one body. It's neat to look at all of the parts. The actions may blow you away because God creates awesome works. Sometimes positions change and you may receive more

Open H†S Word

responsibilities than you thought you would have. Pray about it and follow God's instructions.

Chapters 15-29 Father God looks at the heart. You may be a wholehearted follower of Christ, but if you do things expecting a blessing, I think that's dangerous. When circumstances seem impossible, the Holy Spirit gives you power to complete God's will. The Lord's promises never fail! Satan will put up roadblocks to try to stop you from traveling the Father's journey for your life. Continue to seek God, do His will and be humble!

End of 1 Chronicles

2 Chronicles

Chapters 1-7 The presence of the Lord is such an indescribable feeling and experience. When a person is praying and forgets about the surroundings, he or she can deal with many things that are on the heart. Listening to God may be difficult, but it's worth it.

Chapters 1-7 God the Father wants His children to wholeheartedly seek Him. When you put Him first and at the center of your life, He will mold you into His image! The Lord Almighty sees your heart. When you seek Him, He'll bless and amaze you so pour your heart out to God!

Chapter 8-14 When you don't understand the trial that you are going through, seek God because He is always there. He will help you fight your battles. Be bold and courageous because getting out of your comfort zone helps with your relationship with God. Don't worry; He will give you the words to speak.

Chapters 15-25 For a long time I used to think my loved ones' sins were my responsibility. It was a burden to carry that around. If you have this mindset, God shares fantastic news! Everyone is accountable for his or her own sins. "Yet he did not put their children to death, but acted in accordance with what is written in the Law, in the Book of Moses, where the Lord commanded: "Parents shall not be put to death for their children, nor children be put to death for their parents; each will die for their own sin." (2 Chronicles 25:4) Live like Christ and seek Him wholeheartedly. Christ-like actions will expand the kingdom!

Chapters 15-21 Often you become fearful of completing tasks, but God will never leave or forsake you if you wholeheartedly seek Him. You can complete tasks, but our Father will strengthen your heart to fulfill His purpose and He'll reward you. Put God the Father first in your life!

Chapters 23-36 Good intensions are given, but in trials a person can snap to the point of he or she may become more distant. People may try to put doubt in your faith because they may not believe in God. Sometimes God will kind of "sit back" to know what is in your heart. Prayers maybe answered quickly or slowly, but whatever speed it's time for rejoicing! Always follow God!

Chapters 26-33 Our Father blesses His children when we wholeheartedly seek and praise Him. When God blesses and gives us success, praising and giving Him the honor is easy. Sometimes the success that the Lord blesses us with can be our downfall because we'll think our strengths and abilities are what gave us our success. Staying fearful, obedient, humble, and seeking our Father are what He wants. If you don't, He'll not bless you. Sometimes the Lord leans back to watch and know what's in your heart.

End of <u>2 Chronicles</u>

Open H†S Word

Ezra

Chapters 1-7 The pressures of the darken world can control people. It's important as Christians, to stand up for what we believe. Worship is personal and needs to not waver. Forget about your surroundings. Being a pleaser of men instead of God isn't satisfying. Sometimes turning down help may be needed so God can work out His plan.

Chapters 1-7 You may allow others or fear to control you. All you need is to have confidence in the Lord and press on when you're afraid! Our Father will supply for your needs and go beyond them if you wholeheartedly seek Him. He'll bless you with joy! But others will try to stop you from fulfilling God's will. Don't be troubled. God fights your battles! Continue to seek Him and study His Word. With God Almighty, you're best days are ahead of you!

Chapters 8-10 It's easy to mess up in life. Studying and memorizing God's Word are extremely important. There are times to speak out the Word for correction and times to be silent.

End of Ezra

Open H†S Word

Nehemiah

Chapters 1-7 Dreams can be positive and God is the One who will help you succeed. The first thing to do is to pray about it. Time may elapse for many years before the dream begins to take shape. Sometimes telling your dream to someone may be needed to start your dream journey process. Opposition will come so you need to be on guard all of the time. Pray for your enemies.

Chapters 8-13 Sometimes God's Word needs to be taught by His children to others. He will give the words to teach. Worshipping God is a reflection of how you live your life. Correction may be needed from time to time because people forget things easily. Communicate with God about everything because He is always ready!

End of Nehemiah

Open H†S Word

<u>Esther</u>

Chapters 1-7 There are situations in life where the positives cannot be found right away. Stand firm and do what's right! God is making you stronger.

Chapters 1-7 News spreads and if you aren't doing your job, you'll get fired. You may have to be the kind of person who the Lord chooses to use to correct situations. Of course, fear and terror will set in! By the Holy Spirit, God Almighty will equip you for the task! Seek God and stand firm in your beliefs no matter how the storm rages. God is on your side! Evil won't prevail. Our Father always wins and blesses His children when they wholeheartedly live for Him!

Chapters 8-10 A person has decisions to make. Evil schemes may be overheard and the schemes may be a result of jealousy or a prideful heart. The person who overheard the conversation about the evil scheme has a choice to make whether to ignore it or to avoid it from happening. The prideful person may try to intimidate the morally correct person. If the morally correct person stands firm that will bug the prideful person to no end. Stand firm and do what's right! God is making you stronger! God will make the hardships become transformed into victories and blessings!

End of <u>Esther</u>

Open H✝S Word

Job

Chapters 1-7 God is pleased when His children fear (respect) and honor Him. He will speak well of you in Heaven if you worship Him with everything. Speaking about Him in conversations is such a blessing. Satan does not like it when God's children are devoted to God. Satan will do everything and destroy God's blessings to get you to turn away from God. Your loved ones may think that you deserve this trial and may want you to give up on God. There will be "not understanding" times but you have to always trust, obey and follow God no matter what.

Chapters 8-14 People may think that you deserve the trial that you are in for many reasons and may say it to your face. Others may think that you don't deserve the trial. The person who is in the trial is vulnerable and may be tempted to say negative things quicker. Sometimes a person needs a listening ear and impartiality. Remember life is a vapor so hope in God!

Chapters 15-21 I learned never to judge others' faith. With love and kindness, try to become on their level and explain promises to them or to show how dark the world is. People may agree, but sometimes people need to agree to disagree. Some topics have a never-ending cycle that the conversations are pointless. Someone needs to be the bigger person and stop the conversation.

Remember to fragrance Christ!

Chapters 22-29 When a person asks a question about God, it is neat to give an answer. Listening to another follower of Jesus Christ answer the question may teach you something new and it is a way to know the heart. It may give a clearer understanding and may make you appreciate God even more.

Chapters 30-37 It is easy to think back to the "good old days" during trials. Some people puff themselves up instead of giving the glory to God. Sometimes a person may think that he or she is above God. Whoa, man! If the Holy Spirit puts a word or phrases in you, be bold and speak because nobody is above God! Rebuke this person by showing his or her flaws. Show how God is justice.

Chapters 30-37 Often people think more highly of themselves than they should. They will speak of achievements and most often their loved ones will agree with them. Our Father is the Creator and everyone sins. Be bold and courageous to speak of the Lord God

Open H†S Word

Almighty! God is incredible! Wisdom isn't defined by age. The fear of the Lord is wisdom and to avoid evil is understanding! Obey and trust God!

Chapters 38-42 When God corrects you to put you in your place, your eyes are opened and you realize how incredible God is. God is in charge of many things that a person cannot comprehend. Challenges will arise to know what is in your heart. If you confess and repent that you aren't above God, He will bless you bountifully. Life without God is nothing. When you have accepted Him and start journeying with Him, your life will be joyful.

End of <u>Job</u>

Psalms and Proverbs

I do not outline these books of God's Word because they are above my wisdom and they speak of many circumstances. The book of Psalms has famous Biblical people who wrote this book. They cried and poured out their hearts to God Almighty. They were real and raw with our Lord Jesus Christ. I encourage you to be that real and raw with our Father. The book of Proverbs pens the name of the opposites. It has wisdom on how to act.

Open H✝S Word

Ecclesiastes

Chapters 1-7 It's easy to think that you can take care of yourself. You can decide to put your trust in material items and think that it's going to help for future generations. Life is a vapor. If you have not received Christ as your personal Lord and Savior, you need to because He will bless you. Things will not seem dark or hopeless. He will help if you trust Him.

Chapters 8-12 When you are a new Jesus Christ follower, breaking bad habits may be hard to do. Some of your loved ones may mock your new relationship with Christ. They may try to stop you from building one. You need to remember to be a God Almighty-pleaser not a people-pleaser. Being in a relationship with God changes your heart and outlook on life. Trusting and obeying God is an enjoyable life! The possibilities are endless!

End of Ecclesiastes

Open H†S Word

Song of Songs

Chapters 1-8 When people date, they should be careful in giving their hearts away. Dating is new and exciting, but be aware of red flags. Remember you can't change a person, only God can. If red flags are abundant, get out of the relationship. You are priceless and deserve the best! Couples should be able to give reasons why they love the other person that nobody else can say. Love is special and unique! Once you find it, continue to grow it!

End of Song of Songs

Open H†S Word

Isaiah

Chapters 1-7 We are living in the End Times, but things will become much worse. Products will not sell. Disasters will come and there won't be light. People who don't ask and receive Jesus Christ into their hearts have a rough time living. Satan has a grip on unsaved people that they put their trust in worthless idols. They are so lost and blinded that they think they don't need God and mock Him. As stewards of Christ, spread the fruits of the Spirit around and God will do the rest!

Chapters 8-14 God will make someone to govern the unsaved people. This person will try to lead people to Christ. Some people will run to Christ when they see the banner. Others will be hardhearted and still mock God. God has a plan and will carry it through completion! Remember you can't hide anything from God because He knows everything.

Chapters 15-21 When God reveals something, it's mind blowing! Jesus is the One who will judge people on Judgment Day. (Isaiah 16:5) Actions will be judged so live how you want to be judged by Jesus. Every knee shall bow and every tongue will confess that

Jesus is Lord. The Maker of the universe! The earth will vanish and God's children will worship together without religion in their hearts. Jesus is coming back! Are you ready?

Chapters 22-29 In the world, people are selfish. Their minds are self-centered. They will store up things and may think that they are better than anyone else. In God's timing, the proud or arrogant people will not have authority, but the humility people will be in roles of major responsibilities because God will place them there. The world will be divided. The unsaved people will be consumed by their idols, but God will destroy them. God's children will worship the Lord. There will be no more pain and no more suffering! God's children are like vineyards. God protects His children and shapes them into His image. His children are partners with Him.

Chapters 30-37 People tend to worship the Lord with their mouths instead of with their hearts. Sometimes a person can fool others, but this person can't fool God. He knows everyone's hearts. Worshipping God is a lifestyle. God may tell you to do something

Open H†S Word

that maybe difficult, but obey Him. His plan is far better than yours and He will bless you.

Chapters 38-45 When God reveals something to you, be careful to share it. God may want you to keep it to yourself. He may give an opportunity to share it at a later time, but wait for God's instructions. In the wrong moment, sharing it ruins the blessing. When you are in a trial, it should be a time that deepens your relationship with God. Find the positives in it. Wholeheartedness is what God wants His children to be toward Him. Even though your loved ones haven't traveled down the same path as you are on, trust God's lead because He won't let you fall or fail.

Chapters 46-53 Some people try to act in a certain way around different groups of people. God knows each one of us better than we know ourselves. He is always with us no matter if we are in a calm moment or in the raging seas. God has a plan so follow Him because He may use you to expand His kingdom. He will receive all of the glory! Speak about God out loud!

Chapters 54-61 Idols are worthless so get rid of them because you are angering God. In the world, people want to be loved for who they are. God loves you for who you are and more than you can understand! He loves you more than your loved ones. If you think about what He did on the cross, it may bring you to tears. He comforts you. Think about what He has done for you. Praise God because it brings joy. Ask yourself: Can people see Jesus in me? Spread the fragrance of Jesus around!

Chapters 62-66 People seem to be tired because they are trying to control life by themselves. God says that He does not want to be praised one day a week. God wants us to communicate with Him daily. In doing so, God refreshes our souls and brings joy and peace. The Holy Spirit and the Word will not depart from us if we are in relationship with Christ. Take that step of faith and accept Jesus as your personal Savior. Life will be better with Him because He makes all things possible.

Chapter 66 Faith is believing, trusting, and hoping without seeing plans with our eyes. Everybody sins but we have a choice to repent wholeheartedly to God or to continue sinning without a care in the world. Judgment Day is coming and works of the flesh won't cut it. It's what Jesus sees in your heart. Do you mock God or do you

Open H†S Word

worship Him with your lifestyle? The new Heavens and the new earth will be glorious! God's children will live forever with no sense of time; worshipping God forever!

End of <u>Isaiah</u>

Open H†S Word

Jeremiah

Chapters 1-7 God formed you and is with you always. You have to speak the Word when He tells you to. Be bold in doing so because God has a plan and shares the responsibility with His children. God created you and your mouth. The best thing for your lifestyle is to glorify the Lord. Be a witness that God is real to people. With God's help and in His timing, you can help someone turn his or her life around to live for Jesus.

Chapters 8-14 A follower of Jesus Christ may feel as if he or she is the only one living for God in his or her surroundings. Sometimes it feels as if the wicked are gaining and may have authority over you. To you, the situation does not make sense at all. Continue to seek God and pray to Him because He will provide. Boast in God because He turns evil into good. Be firm in the Lord.

Chapters 15-21 No one can stop God from doing what He plans to do. Repent because God's wrath is serious and frightening. He will take everything away from the unsaved because they don't worship Him wholeheartedly. As a follower of Christ, God wants you to speak His Word no matter what the cost is. If you don't, you are keeping a fire inside of you and will become weary. God will strengthen you.

Chapters 22-29 It is easy to think about yourself. As followers of Jesus Christ, we need to and should know the Word extremely well in order to avoid being deceived. The Word is our double-edged sword so ask God to help you use it. Stand firm and glorify God so that you can be His good fruit. The wrath of God brings disaster so build a relationship with God. There are trillions of reasons for why you should. He takes care of you better than you and your loved one.

Chapters 30-37 You don't want to try to stop God's plan from happening because disaster will come upon you. Besides that you can't stop it. God's plan gives hope, a future, and prospers you. Keep your eyes on Jesus and seek His face, not His hands. Soon everyone will know God and He will bless us even more. God is compassionate.

Chapters 38-45 God may ask you to complete a task in order for someone else to complete it to the finish product. The product may become ruined by tempers of other people so that it has to be recreated. You may receive negative comments and become punished. Don't fret. Complete it with a positive attitude. God will send people who will be on your side and to encourage you. Problems may continue to occur. Seek God's counsel to know what His plan is and share it with those who are asking.

Chapters 46-52 People have different beliefs and will stand up for their beliefs. If the beliefs are not found in the Word and don't line up, the beliefs are nothing. Excuses will be made to protect the beliefs, but we have to follow what God says. It's easy to believe in or take things at face value about what others say about certain scripture verses when you haven't studied the Word yourself. Disaster will come to those who don't wholeheartedly believe nor follow God. The Word is our battle weapon.

Chapter 52 When things around you seem as if you are in the center of a disaster, create an ambush for God to deliver you from the crazy nonsense. Satan and evil spirits have no mercy. They will lead you to death. God will protect you according to His plan. Follow God because people will payback, but they may be doing it with wrong motives. Seek and listen to God.   End of Jeremiah

Open H†S Word

Lamentations

Chapters 1-5 Living day-by-day without Jesus is sadness. You may feel as if you are in a battle. Fighting enemies is tiring and at some point tears may become shed. Loved ones can't help you and may turn their backs on you. "Because of the Lord's great love we are not consumed, for his compassions never fail. They are new every morning; great is your faithfulness. I say to myself, "The Lord is my portion; therefore I will wait for him." The Lord is good to those whose hope is in him, to the one who seeks him; it is good to wait quietly for the salvation of the Lord."" (Lamentations 3:22-26)

End of Lamentations

Ezekiel

Chapters 1-7 The Holy Spirit is a guide for believers to know what God wants them to do or what not to do. He will instruct God's children to speak and act boldly. Don't miss the opportunity to perform on God's behalf because you will regret not obeying God. Forget about what others will think and say because pleasing God should be your number one priority. Be ready for Judgment Day. We don't understand everything, but God's plan will be completed.

Chapters 8-14 Many people think that their actions are hidden in secret. Nothing is hidden from God because He sees, hears, and knows everything. God knows people's hearts, so flattery means nothing. As followers of Christ, rise up and show the world Christ. Will you stand firm in your beliefs even if you're the only one following the Holy Spirit completing God's will? Obey Him in the good and bad times. Actions speak louder than words. It's better to act in helping others than not and regret it later. Everything is for a purpose.

Chapters 15-21 God wants His children to be on fire for Him. Being a fence walker won't cut it. You have to be all in or nothing.

Open H✝S Word

A fence walker is useless. God sees every pain that you are going through. If you make a decision to accept Him as Lord of your life, He will begin to cleanse you and make you new. His love is so great! This is a life journey so don't walk away when it's hard. God is molding you so don't let gossip ruin His masterpiece. Everyone is responsible for his or her own sins. God doesn't want anyone to go to Hell. God gives many chances so repent and live a glorifying God life.

Chapters 22-29 People should think about their actions before completing them. Try to ask yourself this question. Am I glorifying God if I do this? If you will not be, don't do it. Many people need to avoid following in someone else's footsteps because disappointments and struggles will be harsher. God needs to be number One in your life. If He isn't, He will destroy everything. Church buildings should not be so spectacular that the buildings take away the focus on God. Focus on worshipping God.

Chapters 30-35 God created the earth to be good and perfect. God created us to fellowship with Him. The decisions made back then and the decision made in the present day make change. Detestable actions lead to Hell. Once God's plan is completed, He will gather His sheep and make everything right. Make a choice and live out that lifestyle because being a fence walker means nothing. Stand up for what's right.

Chapter 36 Some people enjoy seeing others hurting because they are hurting themselves. They may seem as if they are there for support, but deep down they are glad for the hurting. God isn't fooled and will save you. Disasters will come to those who are not respectful of God's Holy Name. He will gather His children and bless them according to His will because He knows everything. God says, "I will give you a new heart and put a new spirit in you; I will remove from you your heart of stone and give you a heart of flesh. And I will put my Spirit in you and move you to follow my decrees and be careful to keep my laws. Then you will live in the land I gave your ancestors; you will be my people, and I will be your God. I will save you from all your uncleanness." (Ezekiel 36:26-29)

Chapters 38-45 In the world, there are people who sabotage others. If you examine these kinds of people, you may see the hurt that they carry around. God wants you to drop your hurt so that He can lavish everything that He is and far more that no one will understand. Disasters will come to those who are not respectful of God's Holy Name, do not follow Him, and complete detestable actions. Turn from these actions and accept Christ because He wants to bless you. Open yourself up to Christ so His glory can shine!

Chapters 46-48 Decisions have positive and negative outcomes. God wants to bless you because His Son paid the ultimate price by dying on the cross. We don't have to give continual sacrifices or have a middleman to speak to God for us. We have the privilege communicating to God ourselves about whatever and whenever. Respect has to be involved in some level. Ask God what He wants you to do. By asking and completing the action, you are doing His will.

End of Ezekiel

Daniel

Chapters 1-7 Authorities have the power to change systems. They may have the idea to change everything about you. Seek God's guidance because He will orchestrate actions that benefit you. People who work for authorities will sabotage you because of your faith and confidence in God. Stand firm and speak whatever God lays on your heart because He has a plan. You may be put in dangerous circumstances, but God will save you if you are wholeheartedly journeying with Him through life. You can tell when He wants you to speak and when the word is just for you. Chapter 8-12 Often people become scared of the unknown. Sometimes God leaves you guessing in order for His plan to work out. He uses anything to answer you so be alert. God knows your heart. Be humble and glorify God in life. Continue to speak the truth no matter what because God will speak through you. He may reveal things that no one understands.

End of Daniel

Open H†S Word

Hosea

Chapters 1-7 Whatever God says, goes! God will destroy everything when people aren't for Him or seeking Him wholeheartedly. He loves you, wants the best for you, and will take care of you. Don't half-heartedly follow Him. Trials are tests and can temp you to walk away from God. Doing religious traditions or sacrifices don't do anything good if your heart isn't right. God sees your heart's desire that moves by compassion.

Chapters 8-14 Many people think that circumstances work out by their own strength. They will complete rituals that seem pointless to outsiders. When you have accepted Christ as your personal Lord and Savior, it is incredible to see God's tender love and kindness was with you at your youth. God was there from the beginning of time and Jesus created the earth. People say that coincidences happen, but it's God's timing who pours out blessings in which, things fall into place. This will continue throughout your journey with Him! His arms around you is the best feeling! God wants you to consult with Him first before you do anything. God will do

Open H†S Word

anything and everything that He wants to. It's your choice to receive blessings or drawbacks.

End of <u>Hosea</u>

Open H†S Word

Joel

Chapters 1-3 Disasters are coming because we are living in the End Times. Everything will be dry and cut off. God's children will be gathered and they have an idea of what the signs look like. Some people think that they can get God back. They are only hurting themselves. You can't hurt Him. Seek God and let Him be in control of your life. He is gracious and compassionate, slow to anger and abounding in love, and He relents from sending calamity. (Joel 2:13) He will create everything

End of Joel

Open H†S Word

Amos

Chapters 1-9 Often people will think that their actions do not matter so they will do whatever they want. Sometimes the unsaved people will attend church on Sabbaths out of tradition. These people tend to think that church is boring and cannot wait for the service to be over. They cannot wait to go to Heaven and the day that Jesus comes back because they think that it's glorious. This day won't be glorious because crazy weather patterns will happen and people will be extremely afraid. They will experience God's wrath! God's children will experience the glorious events when God allows them to come back to the restoration of everything. The unsaved people will experience disasters because of their detestable actions. They will be thirsty for the Word. Be ready for Judgment Day!

End of Amos

Open H†S Word

Obadiah

Chapter 1 When problems arise, many people won't or don't confront them. Safety and security are things that people strive for. Happiness and to be loved are desires. Often people complete actions to satisfy these desires. God's wrath isn't pretty. What you do, the same behavior will be done to you. Everything is the LORD'S!

End of Obadiah

Open H†S Word

Jonah

Chapters 1-4 Sometimes people try to avoid doing what God tells them to do. They will make excuses and speak to others about the task along with the negative thoughts. Anger and bitterness creates problems when it festers. To speed your journey up, obey God's instructions because His plan is the only one that works. God wants everyone to know His love, kindness and gentleness. Don't hog God to yourself. God wants the unsaved people to repent, turn away from their evil ways and follow Him wholeheartedly. Disasters will be stopped if you give your life over to God.

End of Jonah

Open H†S Word

Micah

Chapters 1-7 People make plans and loved ones can become misleading. Judgment can be sketchy depending on what kind of bribes people are under. That is why it is important to know God and His Word. It's easy to be led astray. God has everything planned out and wants to take care of you. He will defeat your enemies. All that the LORD requires you to do is to act justly and to love mercy and to walk humbly with your God (Micah 6:8). Everyone will know God. It depends on which kind of fear you have of Him that depends on what you will receive. Blessings or disasters. We are in the End Times so live as how you want to be judged.

End of Micah

Nahum

Chapters 1-3 Some people have bullies in their lives. A person may try to stand up to the bully. The standing up action can complete two things. It can make things worse or make the bully stop having the control over that person's life. God will step in and put everything in its' place. "The Lord is good, a refuge in times of trouble. He cares for those who trust in him." (Nahum 1:7)

End of Nahum

Open H†S Word

Habakkuk

Chapters 1-3 A child of God tends to see the wickedness in the world and may complain about it. The world is totally the opposite of what God wants and created it to be. In God's timing, He will recreate everything the way that He wants it. Many people put their trust in idols. Idols aren't going to save or help you so get rid of them. Rejoice and be joyful in the LORD! He should be your strength! He will direct your steps and you will enjoy life. Trials will come, but with God all things are possible!

End of Habakkuk

Zephaniah

Chapters 1-3 The world makes people scared so easily. Putting trust in idols such as stocks, drugs, alcohol, property, and the list could go on, are worldly messages. Idols are material things that won't save people. Jesus is coming back and He is mad when people don't put their confidence in Him. One cause of jealousy is it lashes out so when God is jealous, disasters happen. If people seek righteousness and humility, perhaps they will be sheltered from the LORD's anger. You can't hide anything from God so stop trying. Be on fire for Him! Following God will blow you away. He knows exactly what you need in every season of life. He is always with you!

End of Zephaniah

Open H†S Word

Haggai

Chapters 1-2 Many people tend to be busy in life. They think that their actions will help in the long run. Actions in the wrong way will catch up. People may feel like they can't catch a break no matter which area of life it is. Start focusing on God by building a strong relationship with Him. People can't control life so give up trying. Seek, trust, and follow God because He is in control. His plan is the best and the only one that works! God will ask you to complete actions that you may not understand. Don't fear. Be strong and courageous because He (Holy Spirit) is always with you!

End of Haggai

Zechariah

Chapters 1-7 It is easy for people to play the blame game. Often people blame and hold grudges that they don't see that the problems are self-afflicting. It's time to wake-up and realize that you need to change so do some deep self-examination. Ask God to help you with this. God is a jealous God so be on fire for Him and don't put Him on the back burner. It's marvelous to see God working even though many don't feel as if He is. God protects His children. God is preparing a place for you if you follow Him wholeheartedly. Small beginnings are awesome so don't despise them. God will make things happen for you if you seek and obey Him. ""This is what the Lord Almighty said: 'Administer true justice; show mercy and compassion to one another. Do not oppress the widow or the fatherless, the foreigner or the poor. Do not plot evil against each other." (Zechariah 7:9-10)

Chapters 8-14 As followers of Christ, we have a responsibility on how to act. Others may think that we are strong. Fragrance Christ in His true characteristics tends to make others want to hang out with you frequently. When Jesus comes back, everything will be

Open H†S Word

attractive and beautiful for His children. He will strengthen you in Him if you journeyed through life with Him in every season. Sometimes your loved ones will stab you in the back, so do what's right and put your trust in God.

End of <u>Zechariah</u>

Open H✝S Word

Malachi

Chapters 1-4 People can tell who is following Christ and who isn't. Questions are asked. They may be answered by people's actions. People reap what they sow. It's your choice to seek God wholeheartedly or not. Experience blessings or curses. Some people will deceive you and teach falsely about God. That's why it's important to have a personal relationship with Him so you don't get tossed around all over the place. Guard yourself in your spirit and in faith because Satan will tempt you. The LORD will judge everyone. His children are mold into His image. If you give continuously with the right heart, God will bless you beyond comprehension. Don't cheat God out. Jesus is coming back. Ponder about what you'll say to Jesus on Judgment Day and how you'll live on earth.

End of Malachi

Open H†S Word

Matthew

Chapters 1-7 Often people ponder things for too long. God wants His children to follow Him. He knows what the outcomes will be so that should comfort people. Follow and don't delay. On the other-hand, situations may call for patience. Either way, know that God is working. God's plan works in sequence and His children are apart of it. Of course, Satan will tempt people away from God, but stand firm. Speak the Word out loud because it's a weapon. The Kingdom of Heaven is near! What people think is logical is the opposite of God's guidelines. God is God. His ways are incredible and work for our good and His glory. He looks at hearts so He can't be fooled.

Chapter 1 Some people enjoy figuring out how others are related to them. Jesus Christ lived, died, rose, and lives for us! We are His children and heirs! He has everything that we need and gives it to us! When we seek the Lord God Almighty, He takes care of us. Why not spread and share the Father, Son, and Holy Spirit around in the world?

Chapter 2 God Almighty protects! He knows everything! When His child is in danger, He makes a way out into safety. It will not be a way that seems positive at the time and confusion or madness may settle in. God has a plan and will work everything out for good. Pour your whole being into Him, trust, and obey!

Chapter 3 Many of you think that you have to "do good" actions to receive a ticket into Heaven. Some of you are in the desert for years and these years are when God can teach you or when you're just spinning; not going anywhere. Your heart has to match your actions! Believe in the Lord Jesus Christ and repent! Seek Him wholeheartedly because He is our righteousness!

Chapter 4 Jesus knows what you're going through and has compassion for you. Seek Him and speak to God Almighty about everything. Satan tempts and lies to you. If you wholeheartedly follow God, who He is, is all that matters! Hang out with Him, obey, trust, and read His Word. Live for Christ and act like Him!

Chapter 6 You have to make a choice whether to make your good deeds shown or if you want to be anonymous. God will reward you in His perfect timing. Your body is fragile so guard your heart!

Open H†S Word

Forgive others because Father Almighty forgives you. He will supply for your every need so why not have a relationship with Him? Jesus Christ loves you!

Chapter 7 It's easy to judge others. Instead of judging and thinking that you're perfect, lend a listening ear and share some of your weaknesses. Ask our Father for whatever it is that's on your heart. God sees and hears you. He wants a relationship with you. Throw away your baggage and walk away from the broad path to travel down the narrow road with the Holy Spirit. Build the foundation of life with God to bear good fruit!

Chapters 8-14 Some people have an ego problem. These people tend to think that they have all the answers and their way is the only way that works. Material items can trigger this kind of behavior also. People are prone to setting others on pedestals for many reasons. God says that no one is above anyone. (Matthew 10:24-25) Everybody is the same. God will take care of you because He has your hairs numbered on your head. Don't be afraid to act Christ-like because He will bless you in His timing.

Chapter 8 People interrupted Jesus several times before His death on the cross. He healed the sick, drove out demons, and calmed the raging storm. God, Jesus, and the Holy Spirit wants us to follow Him in all situations all of the time. He is available all of the time so get rid of tight schedules and follow the Holy Spirit's guidance!

Chapter 10 Spread and share the nine gifts of the Holy Spirit with others. Don't be ashamed or embarrass to teach others about the Lord Jesus Christ. Stand firm, be bold, and shine Christ's light! This world is dark and is darkening. If you have a relationship with Christ, He says not to worry about what to say because the Holy Spirit will help you. God knows where your faith level is.

Chapter 12 Studying and spending time with the Lord Jesus Christ are what He desires, but doing it out of guilt or going through the motions are not what God wants. He looks at the heart. Seek God and act Christ-like. God won't give you more than what you can handle! Trust Him and build your faith with Him.

Chapter 14 We don't know God's plan for our lives. In the fuzzy moments, doubt begins to settle in and questions arise, which may cause overwhelming feelings. Every moment of our lives, God wants us to pray and talk to Him. He'll provide for our needs. Don't doubt! Our God saves!

Chapters 8-14 In today's culture, many people have forgotten what the Sabbath is truly about. It's about focusing, worshipping God and taking a rest from schedules. It's a time to complete a good action and God will lead you to that good action. "Anyone who speaks a word against the Son of Man will be forgiven, but anyone who speaks against the Holy Spirit will not be forgiven, either in this age or in the age to come." (Matthew 12:32)

Chapters 8-14 Flattery and having a half-heart for God won't work. Your words and actions show what is in your heart. Living life on earth is a reflection on how you will be judged and what you will receive. Satan will try to stop you from doing God's will. Stand firm and press on. Faith moves mountains. Humble attitudes are what God wants to see to do His will. He loves and cares for you! He will pick you up when you are lost and are finished controlling your life. He rejoices when you come to that realization of you need and want Him!

Chapter 15 It's easy to fall into and follow religious traditions. Many of us don't understand the meanings behind the traditions half of the time. We're going through the motions and know the specific words to say. Our hearts are far, far, far away from God and we don't even know Him. Seeking Father Almighty wholeheartedly is what He desires! He'll begin to change you from the inside out. Your faith and relationship will grow stronger! Your heart is a treasure!

Chapter 16 We wrestle with the topic of faith because of the many viewpoints that are in society. Viewpoints can be like yeast. If teachings and beliefs don't line up with the Holy Bible then they're useless. There are evil spirits who want to throw us off the narrow path. Jesus gives His children power and authority to tell them to leave! Time is precious and winding down. Seek, follow, trust, and obey God before it's too late!

Chapter 18 Children are precious. They trust and don't have set schedules. We are to be as children in God's Kingdom. We should act, as if we don't need to impress or care about others' opinions. We should be seeking God and aiming to please Him. He and the angels rejoice over you when you realize you need Him! Life isn't easy, but with God all things are possible! Love, have mercy, and forgive others as our Father Almighty has forgiven!

Chapter 19 Sometimes God's plan is for you to be single so that He can use you more on a deeper level than married people. Your focus and desire are on Father God Almighty so following Him is easier.

You can pray throughout your day as if you're having a conversation with Him. You can love on people, give encouragements, and give a token of something to be helpful. Being selfish isn't what God calls His children to be. Love richly and help in all situations daily! Real and true love costs you as Jesus Christ died on the cross for you!

Chapter 20 Everything you do matters so complete tasks to the best of your ability. Jesus will judge fairly because He doesn't show favoritism. God has everything planned out and His timing is perfect! Submersion baptism signifies a person being dunked under water getting rid of all the heavy baggage and coming out of the water becoming new in Christ. God changes your heart to have the desire to seek and live for Him. He grows your faith and relationship. As you grow in love with God Almighty, you'll want to serve and bless others as God allows you to!

Chapter 21 Who are you completing tasks or good deeds for? For God or the approval of people? Sometimes an idea springs forth, but the location isn't the best to do it at. Double-check your heart and motives. Don't complete the task if your heart and motives are wrong. Pray in all things and don't doubt. God won't leave or forsake you so put your hope and trust in Him instead of people. They'll disappoint you. Be broken and cling to God so He can make you new!

Chapters 15-21 Sometimes God's children do not want to ask God for their wants for different reasons. Ask God because He wants to bless you. Faith is believing and trusting. Desires should be according to God's will. God will take care of things so that you don't have that burden. Follow Jesus. He wants your heart devotion, not sacrifices. In the world, God's children are sporadically seen. Rise up and stand firm to do what God tells you to do. Freely you have received, freely give. Don't worry about what to say, God's Spirit will speak through you. Wisdom is proved by actions. Judgment Day is near.

Chapters 15-21 When two or more of God's children are gathered together, God is with them. Sometimes forgiveness and being merciful are hard actions to complete. Whatever decision you choose, God will treat you the same way as you are treating your loved ones. God loves us all the same, but blesses us differently according to His plan for our lives. Pray wholeheartedly. God is here for you. Your relationship with God should be both of you giving and receiving.

Chapters 15-21 If you believe and accept Jesus wholeheartedly, He will begin to mold you. Molding is a process that the sculptor takes the time to make every detail just right for satisfaction. Jesus says, "Therefore I tell you that the kingdom of God will be taken away from you and given to a people who will produce it's fruit [acting in the characteristics of God to the world]. He who falls on this stone will be broken to pieces, but he on whom it falls will be crushed." (Matthew 21:43-44) Work with God to break you in pieces no matter what because the transformation is incredible! It's worth journeying with God in life! If you don't believe nor accept Jesus wholeheartedly, you will experience eternal fire. The choice is yours.

Chapter 22 Examine your heart and life because there aren't backdoors to get into Heaven. No one will sneak in or else he/she will be thrown out. No married couples are in Heaven. We'll be as like the angels. Ask yourself this: do I really love God with all my soul, mind, and strength? Is His love overflowing into all aspects of my life?

Chapter 23 Special regulations are crippling people. Religions have regulations and many people having church titles can walk with high prestige that make others want to be as they are or turn them away. Regulations aren't what God Almighty wants. He wants your heart and have you living for Him! He wants you to talk to Him throughout your day, building a solid relationship. Humble yourselves under His mighty-hand and He'll exalt you! Boast in the Lord!

Chapter 24 The End is still to come, but are you ready? Loving people will be rare, but Christ commands us to love. Take a stand

Open H†S Word

in what you believe in and know to be the truth! Deceivers are out there so study the Word and pray yourselves. Continue on the straight and narrow path, which leads to life eternal! Jesus is coming back!

Chapter 25 Our Almighty Father wants His children to be prepared for Jesus when He comes back. We don't know the day or hour it'll be, but soon He's coming with His angels! Are you relying on God, building your relationship with Him, helping, and having compassion for others? Now is the time to act not later because later will be too late! Be servants of Christ to receive a "well done, good and faithful servant" from our King! Being thrown into Hell is the second option. It's either Heaven or Lake Of Fire.

Chapter 28 Christ teaches us how to live, but are we listening and applying it? Are you truly ready for Him to come back and would you recognize Him if He stopped you? I know speaking of Him is scary, but stir up that holy zeal and take a stand! The Holy Spirit is with you so proclaim about God our Father until the end! Don't allow others to stop you!

Chapters 22-28 Gathering together and fellowshipping is fun. Sometimes awkward moments spring up, such as a few people who aren't invited show up. They will be thrown out. If God doesn't know you because you didn't accept Him, He won't accept you. Follow and do God's will. Let love for God be overflowing so that it reaches to others. You have one Father so be careful of what you call the men in your life. The exalted will be humbled and the humbled will be exalted. Faith is tested, but whoever stands firm to the end will be saved. Be alert and watch for signs of the End Times. God's children have clues so don't be fooled. The spirit is willing, but the body is weak.

End of <u>Matthew</u>

Open H†S Word

Mark

Chapters 1-7 God writes His children's testimonies. It's neat to hear what dark-hole they came from to when they accepted Jesus. As your relationship with God grows, you will begin to take steps of faith that may not make sense to outsiders. Share testimonies and let God do the rest. God plants and grows seeds. God allows you to make your choice to have His seeds spring up or not. Satan will try to destroy them. Spread the Word around so that God's kingdom can expand!

Chapter 1 Often we don't know our purposes in life and circumstances may not turn out the way that we expect them to. The great plan may be sitting in a lonely place so that God can build your faith. Spreading the Word of God is what we should be doing by our actions: being compassionate toward one another. We need to pray and be quiet when we know that we should.

Chapter 2 Struggles spring forth, but how you deal with them is the key. Be determined to seek our Lord Jesus Christ. Questions and doubts can arise so talk about them. Check and double-check your life with God.

Chapter 3 People choose to not like others for various reasons. You can choose to put your confidence and draw from God's mercy/strength or curl up under pressure. You have to decide what's important. Make a lifestyle change if need be and be ready for criticism from people.

Chapter 5 How long will you put up or try to make things work on your own? Our Lord Jesus Christ is right there waiting for you with open arms! Put your faith in Him and He'll provide for your needs! Tell the world about our Lord Jesus Christ! He frees you from sufferings!

Chapter 6 People wear masks, but it takes a mature and confident person in the Lord to live out his or her faith in front of others no matter what the conditions are. Be ready for persecution, but don't worry, God is building your character. You may be tired, but call out to God for strength! He will do miracles!

Chapter 7 Worshipping our Lord Jesus Christ should come from the heart and display what's in it. Falling in love with our Lord Jesus Christ and following/obeying Him are what He desires, not

Open H†S Word

phony traditions! Turn your eyes and hearts upon Him! Everything will change for the better.

Chapter 8 Rules are set in this world so they train us as if we're robots; not thinking, but following orders. Wake up and take a stand for God! Shed that robot shell and realize God created creation through Jesus! Nothing, not a single thing in the world can satisfy you. Chose God Almighty!

Chapter 10 In public, it's easy to appear spiritual, but at home can be a different story. God blesses His children with more than enough! Follow Him wholeheartedly because all things are possible with Him!

Chapter 11 Our Lord Jesus Christ prepares everything so all that we have to do is listen and obey. Many people don't rest from their busy schedules. Relaxation is needed and it's a time to refocus on praying/talking to God! Forgive others, pray, and don't doubt. Ask for whatever and you may receive it if it's God's will. People will question you so it's important to know your beliefs and advocate for them. But sometimes silence works better and the Holy Spirit can do what God wants!

Chapter 8-14 We can forget what God has taught us throughout our journey with Him. Analyzing situations can be bad because doubt and fear settle in. Routines settle in and many of us don't realize that we are slipping away from God. Just going through the motions. Ask God for what is needed to have the zeal in your relationship back again. Freshen up your prayers. Be salt and light in the world. Don't doubt and forgive others.

Chapters 15-16 Jealousy can make people complete some crazy actions. If a person confronts the jealous person, the jealous person will deny being jealous. Sometimes actions don't make sense to others. Forget about others and just focus on God. He knows hearts. Live it out by actions. God knows everything before you know and react. As soon as you know that sinned, repent so that you avoid Satan. Show mercy because God has mercy on you. God can accomplish anything if your heart is right with Him.

End of Mark

Open H†S Word

Luke

Chapters 1-7 Prayer is beautiful. People can pray for situations for many years before they receive answers. Sometimes they can doubt the answers because the answers are too magnificent to comprehend. Lessons can be learned at anytime. All that people need to do is be humble and listen. Asking questions is good, but seek God first. God will help you understand. If need be, go somewhere alone to pray if events are too crazy.

Chapters 8-14 A person can have good intensions, but the process of retrieving the end result can be wrong. It can create more problems. A person can make the decision to confront the conflict by taking ownership or can sit there and try to avoid being blamed. These decisions have positive and negative outcomes. Tribulations are tests that will make or break your foundation with God.

Chapters 8-14 God reveals plans to His children in His timing. Following Him is a lifestyle and there is no looking back. People who regret and want to go back to their old life to take care of things are not fit for service in the kingdom of God. Hear the Word and act Christ-like every moment that you are blessed to live.

Shine God's light and love around because this world is evil. People know whom others are living for by actions. "For where your treasure is, there your heart will be also." (Luke 12:34) What or who you love will be evident by your actions and speech. Love God then proclaim it with passion!

Chapters 15-21 God's desire is for everyone, it does not matter what people's backgrounds look like or race, He wants everyone to be saved. He and the angels in Heaven rejoice over people who make the decision to walk away from the darken world and surrender all control to Him! When people make this decision, they need to know that God is always with them and everything that He has is theirs. "For the Son of Man came to seek and to save what was lost." (Luke 19:10)

Chapters 15-21 Honesty is the best policy. Whoever is honest with a little will be trusted with much. Whoever is dishonest with very little will be dishonest with much. The honor system is highly valued with God. God knows hearts and the motives behind actions. Don't be a people-pleaser. Be a God-pleaser because what is highly valued among people is detestable in God's sight.

Open H†S Word

(Luke 16:15) If you have unsaved loved ones, pray for them and be Christ-like to them. Be alert at all times because God sets up moments for you to minister to them. Don't shove Christ down their necks because that will turn them away. Pour God's love and the fruits of the Spirit onto them. Let God create the moment for ministering. Be stewards of the Word.

Chapters 15-21 The kingdom of God is within followers of Christ. His children know what unforgiveness does to them. It creates barriers in relationships and lets Satan have control over your life. You have the decision to confront people to talk it out. You can make the decision to forgive with God's help and pray blessings over them after you have repented about your negative attitude. Be mindful about what you are praying about. Don't think that you're better than everyone else or have all the answers. Be helpful and stay true to whom you are because justice will come in God's timing.

Chapters 22-24 When people do not control their emotions, they tend to regret the impulse decision. They may try to go back and fix it, but it's too late. People can repent and ask God for help. God knows people's life plans before people experience the seasons. Sometimes He sits back and watches what His children will do. He may want a gentle attitude preaching about Him instead of the booming attitude.

End of <u>Luke</u>

Open H†S Word

John

Chapters 1-7 Jesus created the world. The Word has been here since the beginning. God's light or spirit is inside of us. Whoever believes in Jesus Christ have the right to be called children of God. Others hurt often people because their trust in people is created too much. Put your trust in God and live life experiencing Him writing your testimony.

Chapters 1-7 Living a life that truly glorifies God is incredible and beyond one word to express it. I always try to glorify God with my life. Whenever loved ones compliment me, I try to communicate John 3:30 which states, "He must become greater; I must become less." Worship God in spirit and in truth. Let the spring of water that is inside of you overflow into all aspects of life. God will give you the words to speak because He sent you on the journey.

Chapters 1-7 The stresses of the world can weigh people down. Sometimes children of God decide to turn their back on God because of trials. God is molding and getting rid of junk that's inside. This is a process and God will bring it into completion when He's ready. Don't give up. Jesus says what is His is ours. He has blessed and continues to bless His children. Testify about Him. Follow Him and He will tell you things you need to know. The Holy Spirit will counsel you in truth.

Chapters 8-14 When a person does not know what to say or how to act, pray about it. God will make things happen and may prevent hinders. Satan is a deceiver and will lie to people. Children of God know their Father's voice and know that God hears their prayers. His children are scattered right now, but God will gather them and make them one. Are you ready? Jesus died for His children so that they may have and enjoy life.

Chapters 15-21 Love is an expression of what is in the inside. The world makes love complicated and naughty. Many people do not know what love is or how to love. God's love is always being there, merciful, and patient. This is how we have to act toward others no matter what. Trusting in God is what He wants in our relationship with Him. When you receive Christ, you unite with the three persons, Father, Son and Holy Spirit. God is the Way, the Truth, and the Light!

Open H†S Word

Chapters 22-24 God allows His children to make choices. The choices have positive and negative outcomes. Many people analyze and compare things way too much. God guides and teaches us, but it's how we decipher the teachings is how the outcomes are different. Quit worrying. God just wants His children to seek, obey, trust, and follow Him. Stop analyzing and comparing lives. Dive in and journey with Christ! Fall in love with God!

End of <u>John</u>

Acts

Chapters 1-7 Stand up and boldly speak about Jesus Christ. The Holy Spirit will speak for you if you are a child of God. The name of Jesus is powerful. Jesus can bring blessings beyond comprehension if your prayers line up to His will. Depending on the prayer, God may answer it, but in His timing. When trials come, lean on God because He is fighting for you. Man's power won't win. Seek God always! Children of God should be proud when boasting about Him to people. So what if they don't like you because of your faith. Be a God-pleaser, not a people-pleaser. Your journey with Christ will not make sense all of the time, but obedience pays off.

Chapters 8-14 Often people turn to loved ones for advise. Seek God because He has all of the answers. Speaking in tongues and laying on hands on people are not weird. Jesus sent the Holy Spirit to equip God's children to do His will. Be merciful and compassionate toward others as Christ is. He is our example on how to live life. What would Jesus do in blank situation?

Open H†S Word

Chapters 15-21 Trials come and go, but people have a choice to have a positive outlook or a negative one. When God intervenes in someone's life, He has a purpose that only He knows. God gifts His children with specific gifts to complete His will. God uniquely makes each person. He will equip you in His timing. Follow Him wholeheartedly and obey Him because it's an incredible journey.

Chapters 15-21 Many religions and people think that they have to complete practices in order to receive salvation. "God, who knows the heart, showed that he accepted them by giving the Holy Spirit to them, just as he did to us. he made no distinction between us and them, for he purified their hearts by faith. We believe it is through the grace of our Lord Jesus that we are saved, just as they are." (Acts 15:8-9 & 11)

Chapters 15-21 Standing firm and speaking boldly about Jesus Christ or whatever the Holy Spirit leads you to say can be scary. Trials come to try to stop you from obeying, trusting, and following God in His plan for your life. "Do not be afraid; keep on speaking, do not be silent. For I am with you, and no one is going to attack and harm you, because I have many people in this city."

(Acts 18:9-10) I love when God encourages me to not give up and to strive forward! Don't you?

Chapters 15-21 Life is hard, but with God all things are possible! Prepare for trials and know that God has gone through your trials. He will carry you through if you don't stop seeking Him. Continue to follow Him no matter what. The Holy Spirit reminds and warns God's children. Paul's desire should be the desire for all of God's children. "However, I consider my life worth nothing to me, if only I may finish the race and complete the task the Lord Jesus has given me— the task of testifying to the gospel of God's grace." (Acts 20:24)

Chapters 22-28 When a loved one receives Jesus Christ, no words can express how incredible the transformation is! God will give favor on his or her life. Some loved ones may have a hard time believing that it's the same person. Keep seeking God and mountains will fall. God will speak through you! Always be humble and give God the praise for the wisdom He gave you.

Chapters 22-28 Everything works together for good for those who love Christ. Sometimes people are scared to complete tasks for

Open H†S Word

many reasons. Step out of your comfort zone and complete tasks that you know that God is telling you to do. Think about the needs of others. Stand firm and speak boldly. Often people sabotage others, but may act friendly. Keep on being a child of God and speaking the truth. Knowing who you are in Christ and living life that glorifies Him are essentials to live in this darken world. God sees everything and will bring blessings to you! Life changes, but God remains the same.

End of <u>Acts</u>

Open H†S Word

<u>Romans</u>

Chapters 1-7 When testimonies are spoken, they are often encouraging. God makes all things new. Living life without God is dark. Remember your loved ones don't know any better because their hearts are callused. Don't judge. If you are a child of God, the Holy Spirit will convict you, but your relationship with God needs to be intimate. Everyone will be judged on Judgment Day. God does not show favoritism.

Chapters 1-7 Works are useless in the wrong mindset. It's believing and having faith in Jesus Christ that His grace justifies His children. Grace has been paid for by Jesus' redemption. Everyone falls short of the glory of God, but He knows hearts. His molding process won't stop if your faith does not stop. Faith makes the impossible possible. When all hope is gone, God's glory is brought forth! Repent and strive forward. Your flesh and spirit are at war with one another.

Chapters 1-7 Journeying with God is incredible and His ways are beyond comprehension! God shows mercy when we mess up and gives us many chances to follow Him again if we walk away from

Him. Worshipping God is a lifestyle and is a lifestyle that is opposite of how the world engrains how to act. Live how you want to, but blessings or God's wrath are based on your motives. Don't and stop judging others' faith. Don't exalt yourself. Show love and get on their level to explain what God wants you to explain.

Chapters 8-14 There are two ways of living life: the sinful nature way or by the Spirit. These two ways have different desires in life. Children of God get to share in the sufferings of Christ and also share in His glory. People hope in life. Hope for things unseen and that time cannot buy. Hope in God and wait patiently. Everything God works out for the good of those who love Him. Nothing can separate us from the love of Christ!

Chapters 8-14 Many people do not want to go through sufferings, but children of God are equipped for them. It's called endurance and encouragement of the Scriptures that we might have hope. Throughout this process, the Holy Spirit will unite your heart and mouth to glorify Christ. This happens when your faith is firm. Accept one another as Christ accepted you and spread His love around. Joy and peace come when you hope and trust in God.

Chapters 15-16 God has a plan and some sections will not make sense. The works of the flesh do not work. It's what is in people's hearts that God looks at. God has mercy on who He wants to. Stop analyzing everything because God created everyone unique. Totally surrendering your life to Jesus Christ is the most important decision that you will ever make in your life. God will place His children in your life to deepen your faith.

Chapters 15-16 God will place you where He wants you to minister. Boldly speak and give reminders when loved ones fall to the waste-side. Pray for one another. It's refreshing to hear the final result of a trial. Take time to build friendships and accept them with open arms. Act out the fruits of the Spirit, but be careful so that you won't be deceived. Remember the Word is your battle weapon in life.

End of <u>Romans</u>

Open H†S Word

1 Corinthians

Chapters 1-7 God uses the weak to lead the strong. Boast about Christ because people's power is useless without God. Christ is your strength! Testimonies confirm that the Holy Spirit is in you and you do not lack any spiritual gift. The Holy Spirit will guide you in what to say and do. Conviction will come also. God will reveal things when He knows that you are mature enough. Wisdom and understanding are gained by how intimate you are in your relationship with God. Have the mind of Christ and act Christ-like.

Chapters 8-14 God uses anything that He wants. Planting seeds is what He does and you may be a part of someone accepting Him. Children of God are His Holy temples. Don't live as the world lives. Repent and follow God in life. Judgment Day is near and He will judge everyone. Guide brothers and sisters in Christ who have gone astray back to Him in love.

Chapters 8-14 Don't be a fence-walking believer. "No temptation has overtaken you that is not common to man. God is faithful, and he will not let you be tempted beyond your ability, but with the temptation he will also provide the way of escape, that you may be able to endure it." (1 Corinthians 10:13) Do what is good at all times.

Chapters 8-14 Gifts are what God gives His children and each one is special. Each one has a purpose. The Church needs to be united in order to expand God's kingdom properly. We are many parts, but all one body. Get rid of the division. Do everything in love. "Love is patient, love is kind. It does not envy, it does not boast, it is not proud. It is not rude, it is not self-seeking, it is not easily angered, it keeps no record of wrongs. Love does not delight in evil but rejoices with the truth. It always protects, always trusts, always hopes, always perseveres." (1 Corinthians 13:4-7)

Chapters 15-16 God's call is different for each person. Not everyone will be married and being single allows you to focus on God's will. Your attention will not be divided. Loving and worshipping God is better than knowledge because knowledge puffs up. Sometimes people are watching you so that is why it's important to represent the one true God at all times. Don't lead people astray. Take time to minister to others because it's rewarding. You should not be looking for a repayment.

Open H†S Word

Chapters 15-16 The gifts of prophecy and tongues have a way to be used. These can build people up. Unbelievers will think that believers who use or believe in these gifts are crazy. Use them wisely because God has everything in an orderly way. He will use whatever He wants to melt hard-hearts to worship Him.

Chapters 15-16 God has everything planned for a purpose. Everyone has and is on a different pathway in life. Be careful in choosing your friends because bad company corrupts good morals. Everyone has an earthly body that they are born with. We shall bear witness of acting in the fruits of the Spirit, which are love, joy peace, patience, kindness, gentleness, and self-control. Life is hard, but God has given us the victory through our Lord Jesus Christ! Nothing can defeat you if you don't let it. Live life fully committed to the Lord so that your labor in Him is not in vain (1 Corinthians 15:58)."Be on your guard; stand firm in the faith; be men of courage; be strong. Do everything in love." (1 Corinthians 16:13-14)

End of 1 Corinthians

2 Corinthians

Chapters 1-7 Christ takes away sufferings and stresses. We should stand firm in faith even when we are mocked. Joy and peace God gives. Love and act out the fruits of the Spirit. Don't act like the world acts because that's Satan's game. You should fragrance the only true God and His promises. Be reliable because nobody likes unreliable people. "You yourselves are our letter, written on our hearts, known and read by everybody. You show that you are a letter from Christ, the result of our ministry, written not with ink but with the Spirit of the living God, not on tablets of stone but on tablets of human hearts." (2 Corinthians 3:2-3)

Chapters 1-7 Have the zeal of God always. Let it overflow out of you even in trials to others. Give to others what God has given you. Don't do it reluctantly or under compulsion. Make your mind up so that people can see Jesus in you. Obedience brings an enjoyable life if your motives are right. Remember God looks at hearts.

Chapters 1-7 Some people do not enjoy speaking about their past. We need to in order to have people see what God can do for them.

Open H†S Word

Getting on the same level as people are creates a rapport or a relationship in which, people understand one another's feelings. God will set up the moment in which, you can boast about Him. Just be patient and wait for His prompting.

Chapter 1 You should be courageous to fragrance Christ in this dark world. Living for Christ means that you act differently and you have a glow about you. Shine Christ's Light and be bold in sharing God's testimony.

Chapter 3 Trials are apart of life and often they don't make sense. If you keep your eyes on Jesus, He will mold it into something beautiful. Seek God, go through it, and share it to reveal God's power.

Chapter 5 This earth is our temporary home likewise our bodies. Jesus will judge us on Judgment Day. Will He be pleased with how you shared about Him or not?

Chapter 9 A person who gives without expecting anything is a blessing. God is pleased with this type of attitude and will bless you. If you don't give generously, you won't reap generously. God looks at your heart. Give what God has given you!

Open H✝S Word

Chapter 11 It's not correct and some people may look down upon you for boasting about yourself. Let others boast about you because that's commendable. Share how God lifted you out of valleys. Boast in the Lord! God may use you to strengthen others' faith.

Chapters 8-13 The glory of God should shine! Trials come and obeying God is important. You are in a process of God molding and refining you. It is best that you strive forward because Christ is preparing you for His purpose. Encourage one another and be stewards of the Word. Joy comes when loved ones accept Christ!

Chapters 8-13 When people are strongly proud of something, they will boast about it. Children of God need to boast about the Lord. Study as much as you can about Him and let Him mold you. Act Christ-like, but be bold in speaking about Him. You never know when God will use you to expand His kingdom. Be a walking-build-board for Christ. You never know what you say will impact lives. Speak to help God plant seeds.

Chapters 8-13 Depending on your faith, some people enjoy trials, while others do not. God says, "My grace is sufficient for you, for my power is made perfect in weakness." Have Paul's attitude during trials. "Therefore I will boast all the more gladly about my weaknesses, so that Christ's power may rest on me. That is why, for Christ's sake, I delight in weaknesses, in insults, in hardships, in persecutions, in difficulties. For when I am weak, then I am strong." (2 Corinthians 12:9-10)

Chapter 13 Do you really know the Word? The End Times are coming closer and false teachers are lurking. It isn't enough to be spoon-fed the Word because you can be led astray. Seek God and He will help you understand. Have zeal for God! When a friend's situation is similar to yours, be bold in sharing it. God may use you as an instrument to bring this friend into repentance or salvation. But remember to stay loving and humble.

End of 2 Corinthians

Open H†S Word

Galatians

Chapters 1-6 Satan will try to do everything that he can to avoid children of God from following Christ. It's important to know and act out the gospel so that you don't get led astray. Live by faith because the Holy Spirit lives in you. If you don't, Jesus Christ's death is for nothing. Live by faith, not by sight. If you're putting what you learned into practice, your practices mean nothing if your motive is wrong. It's what is in the heart that matters. You need to just believe.

Chapters 1-6 Don't turn away from God. Look at how much He has blessed you. Don't be a people-pleaser, but be a God-pleaser. Remember when God planned moments for you to speak about Him and how you felt. You are a child of God and an heir. There is freedom in Christ. Stop living as the world lives because you will be burdened. Stand firm in Christ and do everything in love along with the fruits of the Spirit. Speak when loved ones are sinning. We can journey in life together because we are all the same.

Chapter 2 Some traditions are hinders and some people just go through the motions of practicing them. Faith means believing,

Open H†S Word

knowing, and standing firm in who you believe in. Traditions don't reward us to have salvation. Jesus Christ is our salvation! His death and resurrection is our hope!

Chapter 4 Freedom in Christ! Faith expressing itself in love is what counts! Living for Christ and being led by the Holy Spirit gives you confidence to live for God. Seeking God and obeying Him when He speaks will produce or grow the fruits of the Spirit.

Chapter 6 Fearing God is wisdom. Living for Him is marvelous and He will bless you in His timing! If you are on FIRE and not luke warm, your satisfaction is Christ. You won't feel lonely because you know you are God's child!

End of <u>Galatians</u>

Open H†S Word

Ephesians

Chapters 1-6 Blessings are unlimited for those who believe in Jesus Christ. He gives wisdom and understanding to His children. He has given us grace because He loves us. Everything is planned out and believing in the gospel, your inheritance is waiting for you. If you believe, you are marked in Him with a seal, the promised Holy Spirit. The Holy Spirit helps you understand Christ better.

Chapter 2 Loving people is challenging, but expressing God's love unites people! When people allow the Holy Spirit to guide them, God works for His glory. God can do far more than we can understand! You should become rooted in Christ and fellowship with other believers to grasp God's love. His love is wide, long, high, and deep!

Chapters 1-6 Remember when you were not living for Christ? The worries of the world weighed you down. In Christ, there is hope, joy, and peace. He makes all things new, but it's a process. The process is so worth experiencing. God lives inside of you by His Spirit. He wants everyone to know Him. No middleman is needed. Freely and confidently speak to Christ. Knowing His love and who

Open H†S Word

He is surpasses knowledge because you know the fullness of God! "He is able to do immeasurably more than all we ask or imagine, according to his power that is at work within us." (Ephesians 3:20)

Chapter 4 Be very careful of the people that you hang around with. Their good or bad habits can rub off on you. Give thanks to the Lord for all He has blessed you with! Be God's light and an encourager!

Chapters 1-6 Encourage one another and do everything in love. Speak the truth in love so that everyone can mature in faith. Act Christ-like because He is making you new. No more worldly behaviors. Children of the Light live in all goodness, righteousness and truth. Find out what pleases the Lord. (Ephesians 5:8-10) Make the most out of every opportunity. Actions speak louder than words and shows what kind of person someone is. Put on the armor of God daily because we are in battle against the powers of this dark world and against the spiritual forces of evil in the heavenly realms. Always pray!

Chapter 6 Preach God's Word boldly and confidently! Grow in love and in the knowledge of God the Father, Jesus Christ the Son,

Open H†S Word

and the Holy Spirit! Be on fire for God to the point of where persecutions for Christ are joyful!

End of <u>Ephesians</u>

Open H†S Word

Philippians

Chapters 1-4 Suffering for Christ should be joyful. God has a good plan for His children and will carry it on to completion until the day of Christ Jesus. (Philippians 1:6) Trust God because you are here on earth for a purpose so live life by doing God's will. Help one another and act Christ-like in every situation. Be humble so that Christ can be glorified in you. Let Him shine through you.

Chapter 2 People boast about different things, such as education, career, and relationships. Would you let go of those self-boasting and all worldly desires to follow God and His plan for your life? Forget about the past and press on toward your future with the Holy Spirit leading you!

Chapters 1-4 "Forgetting what is behind and straining toward what is ahead, I press on toward the goal to win the prize for which God has called me heavenward in Christ Jesus." (Philippians 3:13-14) People should have Paul's attitude when living life. Pray about everything because God already knows. Journeying in life with Him is incredible because He has been through every valley and been on every mountaintop. He will help and teach you lessons because He is your Father who loves you more than your loved ones. God teaches you how to be content in all situations. He strengthens you!

Chapter 4 Your faith in Christ and His love expressed through you should be what others speak of when they speak about you. Be God's child. People will want to pray blessings for you. Everything was created by Christ and for Him. He is the supremacy! Be firm in what you believe in! In Christ, you're perfect!

End of <u>Philippians</u>

Open H†S Word

Colossians

Chapters 1-4 Living life that is glorifying Christ may result in people speaking about you. Wisdom, understanding, and other spiritual gifts, God will bless you depending on His plan. Jesus Christ created everything by Himself and for Himself. Continue in your faith and help spread God's Word around. Have this purpose in mind. "My purpose is that they may be encouraged in heart and united in love, so that they may have the full riches of complete understanding, in order that they may know the mystery of God, namely, Christ, in whom are hidden all the treasures of wisdom and knowledge." (Colossians 2:2-3) Be careful and study the Word yourself so that you will not be deceived.

Chapter 2 Faith and an intimate relationship with Christ are essential! Be honest with God. He will meet you where you are at and teach you. Let the Holy Spirit guide you. Receive God's love. Don't and stop going through the motions!

Chapters 1-4 Rid yourselves from acting out worldly behaviors. Complete the things that you say that you will do. Don't be a two-faced person. "Therefore, as God's chosen people, holy and dearly loved, clothe yourselves with compassion, kindness, humility, gentleness and patience. Bear with each other and forgive whatever grievances you may have against one another. Forgive as the Lord forgave you. And over all these virtues put on love, which binds them all together in perfect unity." (Colossians 3:12-14)

Chapters 1-4 Positive and negative conversations impact lives. Act Christ-like and make the most out of every opportunity. "Let your conversation be always full of grace, seasoned with salt, so that you may know how to answer everyone." (Colossians 4:6) Pray for others in that they may stand firm in all the will of God, mature, and be fully confident.

Chapter 4 Saying that you'll do something and completing it are two separate actions. Saying things tends to be easy, but actually doing it can be hard. If you believe that you're God's child, let your conversations be about God no matter what.

End of Colossians

Open H†S Word

1 Thessalonians

Chapters 1-5 "Let your life be prompted by faith, actions be prompted by love, and endurance inspired by hope in the Lord Jesus Christ." (1 Thessalonians 1:3) The Holy Spirit convicts bad behaviors in God's chosen people. Be a model of Christ in every circumstance including trials. By this, you are helping to expand God's kingdom.

Chapter 2 Being gentle and nurturing are what stewards of the Word should be. This welcomes people to develop relationships with you. God knows hearts so don't be fake around people. Encourage, comfort, and urge people to live lives worthy of God. (1 Thessalonians 2:12) You should cling to God. View trials as strengthening your faith. After trials, God may use you to share them to encourage and strengthen others.

Chapter 2 Actions and attitudes that are produced out of faith, love, and hope in Christ are satisfying. God blesses you with the endurance to finish! Sufferings are involved, but the hope and joy in Christ outweighs the pain. God has given you power to preach

His Word. Share God, His gospel, and your testimony with others gently.

Chapters 3-4 It's easy to be dependent on others. A person can be too reliant that he or she does not think that he or she can live without this person. This person can lead the friend into bad behaviors that are dishonoring the Lord. "Make it your ambition to lead a quiet life, to mind your own business and to work with your hands, just as we told you, so that your daily life may win the respect of outsiders and so that you will not be dependent on anybody." (1 Thessalonians 4:11-12) Do everything in love. Speak about the coming of the Lord Jesus Christ and the difference between what will happen to the unbelievers and the believers.

Chapter 4 Satan is the tempter and tries to block you from doing God's will. Taking advantage of people, showing off your body, sexual immorality, slander, and etc. are not pleasing to God or the way that God wants you to live. Love and live as Christ does! Live a God-dependence life, not people-dependent.

Chapter 5 Be alert and self-controlled because the Day of the Lord is near. "But since we belong to the day, let us be self-controlled,

Open H✝S Word

putting on faith and love as a breastplate, and the hope of salvation as a helmet. For God did not appoint us to suffer wrath but to receive salvation through our Lord Jesus Christ. He died for us so that, whether we are awake or asleep, we may live together with him. Therefore encourage one another and build each other up, just as in fact you are doing." (1 Thessalonians 5:8-11) Love and live in peace with each other. Be respectful.

End of 1 Thessalonians

Open H✝S Word

2 Thessalonians

Chapter 1 Faith and love should be growing constantly. Persevere in persecutions and trials to have a strong relationship with God. God will bless you for all of the sufferings you went through because He is a just God. On the other hand, He will punish those who do not know Him or obey the gospel. Live life for Christ so that you can get to know Him and complete His calling. "By His power He may fulfill every good purpose of yours and every act prompted by your faith." (2 Thessalonians 1:11)

Chapter 1 Depending on how much faith and love you have in Christ, persecutions won't become a bother, but are something you'll have perseverance in. You'll be counted worthy for God's kingdom for your sufferings. God is just. He repays trouble for trouble and comforts when His children are in grief. Seek and obey God so He can bless you.

Chapter 2 The Day of the Lord is near and God gives His children signs to look for through His Word about this Day. Study and strengthen your faith so that you won't be deceived. Stand firm and hold true to the Word of Life. God wants everyone to have eternal

Open H†S Word

life. Turn your back on Satan so that you can enjoy journeying through life with God. "May our Lord Jesus Christ himself and God our Father, who loved us and by his grace gave us eternal encouragement and good hope, encourage your hearts and strengthen you in every good deed and word." (2 Thessalonians 2:16-17)

Chapter 3 Pray. Pray. Pray. Pray about everything! Pray that the Lord may direct your heart in God's love and Christ's perseverance. (2 Thessalonians 3:5) Don't be lazy or let others complete your work for you. Complete your work yourself so that you are not a burden. There is a line between helping out and being a burden. Warn people of this in love.

End of 2 Thessalonians

1 Timothy

Chapter 1 Help others in love, have a pure heart, a good conscience, and a sincere faith. (1 Timothy 1:5) God will give you the strength to complete the tasks that He called you to do. Grace and mercy will be given when you mess up. Don't give up. Your faith and love for Christ will grow abundantly. Have mercy on others as Christ has mercy on you.

Chapter 1 Live in such a way that you live a quiet and peaceful life. Stand firm in your beliefs. Be Christ's example even in the difficult times. Don't know what to do? Pray and seek God.

Chapter 2 "May you fight the good fight, holding on to faith and a good conscience." (1 Timothy 1:18-19) Many people allow circumstances, such as homosexually and being disobedient to parents, slide on by without standing up. You need to stand up and do what's right so stop conforming to this world. Pray about everything and don't forget to give praise or say thank You to God. Pray for others. Remember don't be angry when praying. Your attention won't be on God and your faith journey will be at a standstill until you forgive. By praying, God wants us to "live peaceful and quiet lives in all godliness and holiness." (1 Timothy 2:2) He wants everyone to come to the knowledge of the truth, which is God Himself.

Chapter 3 Often people follow the examples of others or go with the flow in life. The world has many temptations, but you are never too young to fragrance God! Stand firm in your beliefs and be Christ's example in speech, in life, in love, and in faith! Stay pure in your actions. Christ may use you to lead people to Him!

Chapter 4 Don't be deceived by the worldly behaviors and the false guidance. "For physical training is of some value, but godliness has value for all things, holding promise for both the present life and the life to come." (1 Timothy 4:8) It's easy to believe the negative comments that people say about you. Prove them wrong. "Don't let anyone look down on you because you are young, but set an example for the believers in speech, in life, in love, in faith and in purity. Until I come, devote yourself to the public reading of Scripture, to preaching and to teaching." (1 Timothy 4:12-13) "Be diligent in these matters; give yourself wholly to them, so that everyone may see your progress. Watch your life and doctrine closely. Persevere in them, because if you do, you will save both yourself and your hearers." (1 Timothy 4:15-15)

Chapter 5 The world promotes things, such as wealth to make people think that it'll satisfy them. Children of God should pursue righteousness, godliness, faith, love, endurance, and gentleness. Bless and help others out. Put your hope in God! He's our provider of our enjoyment!

End of 1 Timothy

Open H†S Word

2 Timothy

Chapters 1-2 Don't be ashamed of God. Fan the flame of the gift of God. You have God's Spirit of power living in you so boldly live life with sincere faith. You also have the spirit of love and self-discipline. Testify about the Lord and join with the sufferings. Christ is a bodyguard so He won't give us anything that we can't handle. He knows what we can handle and has a purpose. Live life day-by-day and trust God with it because tomorrow isn't a guarantee!

Chapter 1 Sometimes you get too comfortable in your surroundings and let things slide. Burn God's light as a flame and don't let quarrels extinguish it. Satan temps you so that you're not following God. Stand firm and exercise your faith for God's glory! Endure with and for God!

Chapters 3-4 People live how they want to live. More ungodly behaviors are yet to come as the Last Day is near. "In fact, everyone who wants to live a godly life in Christ Jesus will be persecuted, while evil men and impostors will go from bad to worse, deceiving and being deceived. But as for you, continue in what you have learned and have become convinced of, because you know those from whom you learned it, and how from infancy you have known the holy Scriptures, which are able to make you wise for salvation through faith in Christ Jesus. All Scripture is God-breathed and is useful for teaching, rebuking, correcting and training in righteousness, so that the man of God maybe thoroughly equipped for every good work." (2 Timothy 3:12-17) You should be obedient to the Holy Spirit to fulfill God's good plan for your life.

Chapter 4 The Lord will stand by your side and give you His strength to complete His mission. "Preach the Word; be prepared in season and out of season; correct, rebuke and encourage—with great patience and careful instruction. For the time will come when men will not put up with sound doctrine." (2 Timothy 4:2-3) "...Keep your head in all situations, endure hardship, do the work of an evangelist, discharge all the duties of your ministry." (2 Timothy 4:5) The Day of the Lord is near and everyone will be judged. Stand firm and fight the good fight of faith because peace is in the Lord. Hectic is the way the world lives and those who don't believe in Christ wholeheartedly; the wrath of God will disburse. Christ will reward His children who have longed for His appearance.

End of 2 Timothy

Titus

Chapter 1 "…God's elect know the knowledge of the truth that leads to godliness- a faith and knowledge resting on the hope of eternal life, which God, who does not lie, promised before the beginning of time, and at his appointed season he brought his word to light through the preaching entrusted to His children." (Titus 1:1-3) He will give positions to His children. Each one has different responsibilities and rules to follow. Be stewards of the Word to help guide people to be sound in the faith.

Chapter 2 Live a lifestyle that worships God. Teach others about God and His promises. Share testimonies. "For the grace of God that brings salvation has appeared to all men. It teaches us to say "No" to ungodliness and worldly passions, and to live self-controlled, upright and godly lives in this present age, while we wait for the blessed hope—the glorious appearing of our great God and Savior, Jesus Christ, who gave himself for us to redeem us from all wickedness and to purify for himself a people that are his very own, eager to do what is good." (Titus 2:11-14)

Open H†S Word

Chapter 3 "Remind the people to be subject to rulers and authorities, to be obedient, to be ready to do whatever is good, to slander no one, to be peaceable and considerate, and to show true humility toward all men." (Titus 3:1-2) "Warn a divisive person once, and then warn him a second time. After that, have nothing to do with him." (Titus 3:10) Devote yourselves to do what is good in accordance with God's will. Don't live unproductive lives. Chapter 3 Do you gossip, are you quick-tempered, or pursue dishonest-gain? These qualities shouldn't be in a leader. Display actions in hospitable, doing good in every area of life, self-controlled, upright, holy, and disciplined. Actions tend to be remembered more than words. So let God be glorified in you!

End of Titus

Philemon

Chapter 1 Sometimes certain relationships can be hinders. One person can be smothering the other person. The reaction of this is the person distancing himself or herself at arms-length from the smothering person. Time and space are needed for people to change and mature. Separation can be positive. Behavior is the key to show God's love and how much you changed to others. As followers of Christ, we are called to act differently because we are His children. In love, direct people, not force them to God. Exceed their expectations and share the knowledge that Christ has given you, but stay humble.

End of Philemon

Open H†S Word

Hebrews

Chapter 1 Before Jesus Christ died on the cross, He spoke through the prophets in various ways. Jesus Christ died to have a relationship with His children and paid the ultimate price for our sins. He reigns! Angels are ministering spirits. Think about how a fire grows. Wind and flames, right? God's children are the flames and He sends angels who are the wind to help with miracles in His timing.

Chapter 1 Jesus is superior! He is the same yesterday, today, and forever! Think about all that He has done and His love for you. Fan His light in your life!

Chapter 2 Avoid being deceived. "This salvation, which was first announced by the Lord, was confirmed to us by those who heard him. God also testified to it by signs, wonders and various miracles, and gifts of the Holy Spirit distributed according to his will." (Hebrews 2:3-4) Think about Jesus. Crowned with glory and honor because He suffered death to taste it for everyone by the grace of God. Temptations come and Jesus was tempted, but never sinned. So He is able to help His children who are being tempted. Ask and seek God.

Chapter 3 When we worship by giving our time in lending a hand, listening to, and praying for others, we are being the characteristics of Christ and know who He is. "Therefore, holy brothers, who share in the heavenly calling, fix your thoughts on Jesus, the apostle and high priest whom we confess." (Hebrews 3:1) "But Christ is faithful as a son over God's house. And we are his house, if we hold on to our courage and the hope of which we boast." (Hebrews 3:6) It's not easy to be persecuted, but your love for God and hope you have in Him should be evident in your life that you speak of Him constantly no matter what.

Don't turn away from God. "But encourage one another daily, as long as it is called Today, so that none of you may be hardened by sin's deceitfulness." (Hebrews 3:13) Someone can become knocked off God's path little by little. Pray and give a word of encouragement, but don't stop believing that he or she will follow God!

Chapter 4 Faith is believing. "For the word of God is living and active. Sharper than any double-edged sword, it penetrates even to dividing soul and spirit, joints and marrow; it judges the thoughts and attitudes of the heart. Nothing in all creation is hidden from God's sight. Everything is uncovered and laid bare before the eyes of him to whom we must give account." (Hebrews 4:12-13) Your life including your secrets and moments that you're not fond of, Jesus will judge. Boldly and confidently, God wants us to approach the throne of grace because He knows what we are going through. He can help, but we have to ask Him.

Chapter 5 Trials and sufferings are ways to strengthen your faith journey. Some people allow others to complete tasks for them and can make the trial worse by speaking about it. It's time to stop with the elementary ways and grow up. Seek God. He is the only One who can help you. Journey in life with Him so that He can mold you and make your relationship stronger. Let Him begin the transformation so that He can use you to help others.

Chapter 5 Jesus has gone through everything that is a temptation and suffering. Jesus understands what you are going through. He learned obedience as we should, but didn't sin. God wants you to learn and put His Word into practice! Learn in the trials so that God can mold and mature you! Pray constantly!

Chapter 6 "God is not unjust; he will not forget your work and the love you have shown him as you have helped his people and continue to help them. We want each of you to show this same diligence to the very end, in order to make your hope sure. We do not want you to become lazy, but to imitate those who through faith and patience inherit what has been promised." (Hebrews 6:10-12) Don't fall away to begin living as the world lives again. Compare the two lives you lived. Before you surrendered your life to Christ to developing an intimate relationship with God our Father and Jesus Christ.

Chapter 7 When a person helps others who are in need, it changes hearts if the motives are pure. "And without doubt the lesser person is blessed by the greater." (Hebrews 7:7) "But because Jesus lives forever, he has a permanent priesthood. Therefore he is able to save completely those who come to God through him, because he always lives to intercede for them." (Hebrews 7:24-25)

Open H†S Word

"He sacrificed for their sins once for all when he offered himself. For the law appoints as high priests men who are weak; but the oath, which came after the law, appointed the Son, who has been made perfect forever." (Hebrews 7:27-28)

Chapter 7 Lend a hand or be a listening ear. Help others out in ways that blesses them. Show the characteristics of God to others because living for Christ is a joy! God blesses when He sees your heart right! Stand firm for Him so Jesus can intercede for you.

Chapter 8 People make things better for improvement. The Lord has done this same thing with the new covenant. The old covenant was religious practices, like a checkmark list to do. "But the ministry Jesus has received is as superior to theirs as the covenant of which he is mediator is superior to the old one, and it is founded on better promises." (Hebrews 8:6) The new covenant is when Jesus willingly died on the cross. He wants His laws to be in our minds and to be written on our hearts. Believe and accept Christ. Let everyone know Christ through you.

Chapter 9 In the world, there are many religions that have different traditions that are followed. Christ suffered and died once. Often religions tend to be off course in their practices. Study and know God's Word. In context is what gets tricky to not misinterpret scriptures. "Then Christ would have had to suffer many times since the creation of the world. But now he has appeared once for all at the end of the ages to do away with sin by the sacrifices of himself. Just as man is destined to die once, and after that to face judgment, so Christ was sacrificed once to wake away the sins of many people; and he will appear a second time, not to bear sin, but to bring salvation to those who are waiting for him." (Hebrews 9:26-28)

Chapter 10 Have you ever felt as if you weren't doing enough for God? That's works of the flesh. God looks at hearts. Believing and obeying Christ make us made holy through His one time sacrifice on the cross. We are made perfect because of what Christ was willing to do for us: dying for us. When the odds seem to be against you, persevere! "Let us draw near to God with a sincere heart in full assurance of faith, having our hearts sprinkled to cleanse us from a guilty conscience and having our bodies washed with pure water. Let us hold unswervingly to the hope we profess,

Open H†S Word

for he who promised is faithful. And let us consider how we may spur one another on toward love and good deeds. Let us not give up meeting together, as some are in the habit of doing, but let us encourage one another – and all the more as you see the Day approaching." (Hebrews 10:22-25) The Day is when Jesus comes back on earth!

Chapter 10 God's children are called to act differently. Suffer for Christ because He will repay your sufferings with blessings. "So do not throw away your confidence; it will be richly rewarded. You need to persevere so that when you have done the will of God you will receive what he has promised." (Hebrews 10:35-36) Loving people and being merciful when others aren't showing these behaviors back to you is difficult. Be patient and confidently speak the truth of Christ because God knows your heart.

Chapter 11 Not everything can be explained. Stepping forward with God is incredible. "Now faith is being sure of what we hope for and certain of what we do not see." (Hebrews 11:1) "And without faith it is impossible to please God, because anyone who comes to him must believe that he exists and that he rewards those who earnestly seek him." (Hebrews 11:6) Seek God and aim toward the unknown because God will bless you beyond comprehension! Don't dwell. Move forward and look at the positives!

Chapter 12 Many people view discipline as a "bad" action to complete or receive. Think about discipline as a love-training tool for improvement and preparing for the next seasons. "No discipline seems pleasant at the time, but painful. Later on, however, it produces a harvest of righteousness and peace for those who have been trained by it." (Hebrews 12:11) Be thankful and worship God wholeheartedly along with reverential fear.

Chapter 13 Look to believers when your faith needs encouragement. It will strengthen your intimacy in your relationship with God. Remember and put into action the knowledge that God has taught you. Praise God continually. It pleases God when His children do positive activities and share with others. Obey and submit to authorities so that you may be a joy to work with instead of a burden. Have a clear conscience and desire to live honorably in every way. Seek God so that He can equip you with everything good for doing His will, and may He work in us what is pleasing to Him, through Jesus Christ, to whom be glory forever and ever. (Hebrews 13)

End of <u>Hebrews</u>

James

Chapter 2 "Speak and act as those who are going to be judged by the law that gives freedom, because judgment without mercy will be shown to anyone who has not been merciful. Mercy triumphs over judgment!" (James 2:12-13) Be one person who is a child of God. Circumstances change, but don't let the world control you. Don't show favoritism because Christ does not. Treat everyone and everything as Christ does. He is our example on how to live! Chapter 2 It isn't enough to preach faith to others. If you say that you're God's child, show it by your lifestyle. Study God's Word and allow Him to mold you into His masterpiece. Be humble and give God's love, mercy, and a helping hand to others. Stop judging and having favoritism. Start putting God's wisdom into practice! Chapter 3 We are constantly watched. Humility is the best characteristic a person can be. Choose your words because they can either destroy or bring praises. Be someone that people can speak about with similar characteristics instead of living a double personality life. Live out the wisdom that God has taught you. "But the wisdom that comes from heaven is first of all pure; then peace-loving, considerate, submissive, full of mercy and good fruit, impartial and sincere. Peacemakers who sow in peace raise a harvest of righteousness." (James 3:17-18)

Chapters 4-5 Tomorrow is not a guarantee. Make every moment count! "You are a mist that appears for a little while and then vanishes. Instead, you ought to say, "If it is the Lord's will, we will live and do this or that." Anyone, then, who knows the good he ought to do and doesn't do it, sins." (James 4:14-15 & 17) "Let your "Yes" be yes, and your "No," no, or you will be condemned." (James 5:12)

Chapter 4 Many people often live by their feelings. Anger springs forth when a person tries something out of abilities or desires instead of asking God. Submit to God to enjoy life. Life is a vapor so why not do His will for your life. Be helpful. God will give you favor if you're supposed to have it.

<u>End of James</u>

1 Peter

Chapter 1 Unbelievers and fence-walking believers will not have the wisdom, knowledge or understanding as Spirit-filled believers have, which God has given His children. His children should be acting Christ-like and speaking the Word so that God is glorified. Don't shrink back in difficulties. Speak and act out the wisdom, knowledge, and understanding that Christ has taught you. "Therefore, prepare your minds for action; be self-controlled; set your hope fully on the grace to be given you when Jesus Christ is revealed. As obedient children, do not conform to the evil desires you had when you lived in ignorance. But just as He who called you is holy, so be holy in all you do; for it is written: "Be holy, because I AM holy." (1 Peter 1:13-16) With the deepest sincerity in your heart, repent of your sins and believe in our Lord Jesus Christ. The Holy Spirit will help you know what's pleasing to God and you've a choice whether to obey or not.

Chapter 1 Works of the flesh won't do anything. It is through Jesus and His resurrection that His children are saved. "Through Him you believe in God, who raised Him from the dead and glorified Him, and so your faith and hope are in God." (1 Peter 1:21)

Chapter 2 There are two ways of living life. One is when people live in the flesh doing whatever they want. The other is when people live for Christ and they are following His lead by the Holy Spirit. "But you are a chosen people, a royal priesthood, a holy nation, a people belonging to God, that you may declare the praises of Him who called you out of darkness into His wonderful light. Once you were not a people, but now you are the people of God; once you had not received mercy, but now you have received mercy." (1 Peter 2:9-10) "Dear friends, I urge you, as aliens and strangers in the world, to abstain from sinful desires, which war against your soul. Live such good lives among the pagans that, though they accuse you of doing wrong, they may see your good deeds and glorify God on the day He visits us." (1 Peter 2:11-12)

Chapter 2 Sometimes it is hard to submit to authorities. In some instances, people will be sabotaging you. Keep your chin up and seek God. Stand firm in your faith and act Christ-like."...But if you suffer for doing good and you endure it, this is commendable before God. To this you were called, because Christ suffered for you, leaving you an example, that you should follow in His steps." (1 Peter 2:20-21)

Chapter 3 A person's life can seem to have everything going for him or her. A person can have the expensive houses, cars, name-brand clothes, shoes, accessories, make-up, maids, and popularity. People may see that this person is good-looking, talented, fun, nice, and outgoing. Many people look at the outer appearances for beauty. Stop doing that. Beauty lies within hearts so stop commercializing yourselves. "Instead, it should be that of your inner self, the unfading beauty of a gentle and quiet spirit, which is of great worth in God's sight. For this is the way the holy women of the past who put their hope in God used to make themselves beautiful." (1 Peter 3:4-5)

Chapter 3 A testimony that you're God's child is shown through your lifestyle. It's easy to do evil things when you've been hurt. God wants His children to repay evil with good. There's nothing more beautiful than a life transformed and devoted in Christ!

Open H†S Word

Humbly act Christ-like because Christ may be using you to bring people to Himself.

Chapter 5 As children watch how their caregivers act in different situations so do unbelievers watch believers. Love and be hospitable. You are Christ's example to the world. Seek God and don't slip during trials, especially. Think about trials as faith exercises. The more you workout, the stronger you will be. "So then, those who suffer according to God's will should commit themselves to their faithful Creator and continue to do good." (1 Peter 4:19)

Chapters 4-5 Live devoted to Christ that you don't care what others think. They may mock, but God knows your heart. Live humbly and respectfully. God may exalt you because you had suffered when you stood firm in Him!

End of 1 Peter

2 Peter

Chapter 1 People have the ability to forget things. Faith refresher courses should be embraced with wide-open arms. Be honest when you are evaluating yourself and stop evaluating others. Focus on what God is speaking to you and with His help, begin to change. "So I will always remind you of these things, even though you know them and are firmly established in the truth you now have. I think it is right to refresh your memory as long as I live in the tent of this body, because I know that I will soon put it aside, as our Lord Jesus Christ has made clear to me. And I will make every effort to see that after my departure you will always be able to remember these things." (2 Peter 1:12-15) "Above all, you must understand that no prophecy of Scripture came about by the prophet's own interpretation. For prophecy never had its origin in the will of man, but men spoke from God as they were carried along by the Holy Spirit." (2 Peter 1:20-21)

Chapters 1-2 Strive to put God's Word into practice. Read it and the Holy Spirit will remind you of the truth. Don't be a led astray

Open H†S Word

by false teachers. It's time to seek God, dig in, and take action in what you know is true!

Chapters 3 Don't be deceived. "But grow in the grace and knowledge of our Lord and Savior Jesus Christ." (2 Peter 3:18)

End of 2 Peter

1 John

Chapter 1 Don't be a two-faced person. No one appreciates a person who is like that type of a person anyway. In some instances, the actions of the two-faced person will catch up to him or her. Let your actions be the same as you speak. It pleases God when your speech and actions match up and glorifies Him. Don't let peer-pressure change you.

Chapter 1 When you have an intimate relationship with God, your life should display it. Your testimony should be on your lips all of the time and the lessons that He has taught you! If you say that you're God's child, show it by your actions. Don't turn off and on the Light to become a liar. Make a choice. I'm choosing the Light and to shine brightly!

Chapter 2 Sometimes God's children tend to forget that Jesus' death is for everyone. It's all right to personalize His death, but just remember His death is for the whole world. "He is the atoning sacrifice for our sins, and not only for ours but also for the sins of the whole world. We know that we have come to know Him if we obey His commands. The man who says, "I know Him," but does

Open H†S Word

not do what he commands is a liar, and the Truth is not in him. But if anyone obeys His Word, God's love is truly made complete in him. This is how we know we are in Him: Whoever claims to live in Him must walk as Jesus did." (1 John 2:2-6)

Chapter 2 Act Christ-like in all circumstances. Remember what God has taught you throughout your journey with Him. "...Its truth is seen in Him and you, because the darkness is passing and the true Light is already shining. Anyone who claims to be in the Light but hates his brother is still in the darkness. Whoever loves his brother lives in the Light, and there is nothing in him to make him stumble. But whoever hates his brother is in the darkness and walks around in the darkness; he does not know where he is going, because the darkness has blinded him." (1 John 2:8-11)

Chapter 2 The world pushes people and gets them to panic. The world hooks people into things that do not give people a life that is fulfilling. Sometimes when a person reaches a goal that he or she was pursuing for many years, the result is not as satisfying as the person thought it would be. "The world and its desires pass away, but the man who does the will of God lives forever." (1 John 2:17)

Chapter 2 Maturing in your faith takes obeying and trusting God. The time that you spend with God is how intimate God and you will be. "See that what you have heard from the beginning remains in you. If it does, you also will remain in the Son and in the Father. And this is what He promised us—even eternal life." (1 John 2:24-25)

Chapter 2 Be confident and unashamed before Christ at His second coming. Speak boldly to Him and about Him to others. Proclaim His Name because when you do, He is speaking about you in Heaven like a proud parent. Speak and act out what Christ has taught you. "If you know that He is righteous, you know that everyone who does what is right has been born of Him." (1 John 2:29)

Chapter 3 What God's children know and should be proclaiming, the world doesn't understand. Continue to seek God and allow Him to mold you. He is molding you for His purpose in life. Journeying with Him to the end is worth struggling for. When you are standing in front of Jesus, what will He say to you about your life? Will He be proud or disgusted? "...But we know that when He appears, we

Open H†S Word

shall be like Him, for we shall see Him as He is. Everyone who has this hope in him purifies himself, just as He is pure." (1 John 3:2-3)

Chapter 3 When you have an intimate relationship with God, you should pour out onto others the love of Christ. Love and give. It's time to do something! Live, as you're a child of God instead of merely blabbing.

Chapter 5 Pray and love one another. Give correction when needed.

Chapter 5 When you believe in Jesus, He fights your battles. Who the Son sets free is free indeed! Boldly and respectfully ask God for anything. If it's God's will, He will bless you with the request. Press in and press on during trials because God is maturing you!

End of <u>1 John</u>

Open H†S Word

<u>2 John</u>

Chapter 1 As much time spent with God is how intimate your relationship with Him will be. Set your life as a lifestyle that represents Christ. Let the grace, mercy, and peace that you have inside overflow out and onto others. Stand firm so that you won't be led astray. Temptations come to destroy your journey with God. Patience is hard.

Chapter 1 Study God's Word so that you won't be led astray. God desires an intimate relationship with you. God's love is incredible and so once you have experience His love yourselves, shower His love on others! Stand firm in your beliefs and be humble. It's fine to disagree, keep praying.

End of <u>2 John</u>

Open H†S Word

3 John

Chapter 1 Being friendly is sometimes hard, especially to strangers. Some strangers act rude. Keep in mind that they may have had a hard-life filled with disappointments. No one treated them with the fruits of the Spirit. Act out the fruits and over time, with God's help, you will soften strangers' hearts. Be hospitable. Lavish God's love on them so that they learn about God and spread His Word around. There will be hinders to try to stop you. Seek God and press forward!

Chapter 1 Love people as God loves you. Spending quality time with God is how you will get to know Him, Jesus, and the Holy Spirit. Once you develop a relationship, you'll know Him and how to act like Him. Don't act like the world acts. Have compassion for others!

End of 3 John

Jude

Chapter 1 Did you know that you don't need to be in control of your life? Christ wants to have an intimate relationship with you and nothing will satisfy the emptiness in your heart, but the Spirit Himself. Living without Christ leads to corruption and Judgment Day is near. Live how you want to be judged. Live out your faith and God may use you to save others from Lake Of Fire.

End of Jude

Open H†S Word

Revelation

Chapter 1 The Lord is coming back! "Blessed is the one who reads the words of this prophecy, and blessed are those who hear it and take to heart what is written in it, because the time is near." (Revelation 1:3) Every knee will bow and every tongue will confess that He is Lord! Judgment Day is near so examine your life.

Chapter 1 It's funny how people picture God to look like. Try to have and create this picture in your mind of Jesus Christ. "...Someone "like a Son of Man," dressed in a robe reaching down to His feet and with a golden sash around His chest. His head and hair were white like wool, as white as snow, and His eyes were like blazing fire. His feet were like bronze glowing in a furnace, and His voice was like the sound of rushing waters. In His right hand he held seven stars, and out of His mouth came a sharp double-edged sword. His face was like the sun shining in all its brilliance." (Revelation 1:13-16)

Chapter 1 It's often pronounced and misused that God lives inside your heart. God and Jesus live in Heaven on the throne orchestrating everything. If your heart is right (fully devoted to Christ,) the Holy Spirit will help you understand and counsel you to put God's Word into practice in your life.

Chapter 1 God loves you and gave His Son, Jesus to die for your sins! He freed you by His blood! He longs for every person to be in relationship with Him. God knows everything so let Him be in control. Take a moment to picture Jesus. Imagine and absorb Revelation 1:13-16 in your mind. Take a look. Don't be lazy! Jesus is important so look and meditate on Him!

Chapter 2 God sees and knows everything! Stir back up that zeal that you had in the beginning of your relationship with God. Fall in love all over again with Christ because He is your first love! "I know your deeds, your hard work and your perseverance. I know that you cannot tolerate wicked men, that you have tested those who claim to be apostles but are not, and have found them false. You have persevered and have endured hardships for My Name, and have not grown weary. Yet I hold this against you: You have forsaken your first love. Remember the height from which you have fallen! Repent and do the things you did at first." (Revelation 2:2-5) Repent for all of your wrongdoings!

Chapter 2 When you first began a relationship with God, you spoke of Him fondly and were eager to spend time with Him because you were in love and on fire for Him. But as relationships grow, sometimes, some relationships fade away and stop doing what they first did. They become relaxed and may begin to start old habits again when they know its displeasing God. Fall back in love with God and ask Him to help you be on fire for Him because you two know when you're not. Act the way you first acted! Listen to worship music and if you can, sing along and dance to the worship music Pray about everything because God cares about you. Let Christ be your first love always! You should pray and ask God for help first.

Chapter 3 The door to God is always open. Satan will tempt you to walk away from God. The Lord says, "I know your deeds. See, I have placed before you an open door that no one can shut. I know that you have little strength, yet you have kept my word and have not denied My Name." (Revelation 3:8) We can't be and aren't perfect. Patience and persistence in God are what is in needed in life! "Since you have kept My command to endure patiently, I will also keep you from the hour of trial that is going to come upon the whole world to test those who live on the earth." (Revelation 3:10)

Chapter 3 Some people think that attending church and doing church duties is what Christ wants or pleases Him. They may be going through the motions and want others to recognize their name at church. If you're living like this, you're desperately mistaken. Christ desires an intimidate relationship and wants your heart! Out of the heart, the mouth speaks. Don't be a fence-walker. Christ allows you to choose whether you're all in and on fire for Him or if you're of the world and bitterly cold. One day soon, Jesus is coming back so will He call you worthy because you believed, received, heard, obeyed His Word, stood firm, and repented. Repented means you're sorry for the wrongs that you've done. Seek Christ wholeheartedly and do His Word!

Chapter 4 God sits on His throne in Heaven and all of creation worships Him. He will hand the scroll over to Jesus who is the Lamb who is slain because He is worthy to break the seals in order

Open H†S Word

to read it. Instructions and duties will be taken place in order to fulfill the End Times. God's children will be given a white robe because we have been slain for Christ's sake and did not turn away when circumstances were tough. We will have to wait just a little longer until Judgment Day is completed.

Chapter 4 God is in Heaven sitting on His throne. Twenty-four other thrones surround His throne with elders sitting on them. Elders are dressed in white wearing gold crowns. Living creatures sing praises and worship God along with the elders. Give God glory, honor, and thanks! God created everything. Worship God with your whole being!

Chapter 5 Jesus is the Lamb of God. In God's perfect timing, God will allow the Lamb to break and open the scroll. The four living creatures and the twenty-four elders will worship the Lamb. Playing harps with prayers of the saints (Christians) will be the aroma along with incense. Singing praises to God and the Lamb. God will be a proud Father than He already is of His Son. The Father enjoys His children worshipping His Son. I bet He'll be beaming with love, joy, and proudness when this moment comes!

Chapter 6-7 The sun and the moon will be forbid to shine. Four angels will be instructed to block the wind from reaching the earth. Another angel will say to the four angels, "Do not harm the land or the sea or the trees until we put a seal on the foreheads of the servants of our God." (Revelation 7:3) A great multitude that no one will be able to count, from every nation, tribe, people, and language (all of the culture's language in the world), will be standing before the throne and in front of the Lamb. They will be wearing white robes and holding palm branches in their hands. They will be worshipping Christ. The white robed people will come out of the great tribulation. Christ will wipe every tear and there will be no more pain or sufferings.

Chapter 6 When the Lamb opens the six seals, the living creatures assign duties to white, red, black, and pale horses. There will be no more peace, higher costs, kill the earth by sword, famine, and plague by riders on the horses. God's children's souls will be under the alter who have stood firm and been persecuted for their faith in Jesus. They will be waiting for Jesus to judge the world. They will wear white robes when everything is completed. On earth everything will be destroyed and the people who still don't believe in Jesus will want something to hide and kill them from the Lamb's wrath.

Chapter 7 No wind will be blown on the earth because the angels' duty is to have no wind blown. They will not harm the earth until other angels put a seal on the foreheads of God's children. 144,000 children from every nation, tribe, people, and language will come out of the great tribulation. They will believe in God. They'll be worshipping God and the Lamb. The Lamb's blood (Jesus' blood) will make their robes white. God will lavish His love as (I imagine) a warm blanket around them. He promises there'll be no more hunger, thirst, or scorching sun. God will wipe away every tear!

Chapter 8 Jesus opens the seventh seal and there'll be silence in Heaven for a half-hour. Incense and the prayers of saints (Christians) are on the alter. Various weather related storms will transpire, such as thunder, rumblings, lighting, and an earthquake because of an angel will throw down fire from the censer upon the earth. Seven angels will sound seven trumpets that will cause hail, fire, blood, blazing mountain, blazing star, and the solar system will darken to bring destruction upon the earth.

Chapter 9 Locusts prepared for battle will have power as scorpions do to torture people for five-months who do not have God's seal on their foreheads. Locusts will not harm the earth itself. They will sting people to make them suffer and people will want to die. These locusts will have human faces wearing possibly gold crowns. In the great river of Euphrates, four angels will be released when the moment comes to kill a third of mankind. Plagues of fire, smoke, and sulfur will come from the horses with riders. For the rest of mankind who didn't die, they still won't repent for their evil ways.

Chapter 10 Something will happen that God doesn't reveal in His Word. It's a mystery that will happen in God's perfect timing! If God has blessed you with the gift of prophesying (a word from God to comfort or to encourage people), prophesy about many peoples, nations, languages, and kings. Be bold and speak up! If you don't, it will turn sour in your stomach. You'll plus others around you will miss the comfort, encouragement or to be strengthen by the word from God.

Chapter 10 A mighty angel will come down from Heaven holding a little scroll. This angel will stand on the sea with his right foot and his left foot will be on the land. A shout sounding like a lion's roar comes from the angel to get the attention of the seven thunders. We don't know what the seven thunders say yet. The angel standing on the sea will raise his right hand toward heaven to acknowledge God because Christ created everything, will say, "There will be no more delay!" (Revelation 10:6) God's children are to proclaim Jesus in the world.

Chapter 11 God protects His children when they prophesy. Sometimes prophecy is not something that is an encouragement so people will dislike you and sabotage you. You may feel as if the wind got kicked out of you and may become confuse. God will pick you up and dust you off. This type of event will happen in the End Times, but it will be in a different atmosphere. Fear will grip the unbelievers. After this, a city will collapse and an earthquake kills people. The survivors will be terrified and will give glory to the God of Heaven. But God's plan to create the New Heaven and Earth will not be established yet.

Chapter 11 Two witnesses will be prophesying for 1,260 days without harm, but if anyone tries to harm them, fire will come out of their mouths to devour enemies. These men will have power to stop rain from happening while they are prophesying, turn waters into blood, and strike the earth with plagues as often as they want. When these witnesses finish prophesying and giving their testimony, the beast will come up from Hell and kill them. People will be happy that these men are dead and no burial will take place because the torment will cease. But God will bring them back to life after three and a half-days. God will call them home in Heaven after they freak their enemies. A severe earthquake will come and a tenth of the city will collapse. Seven thousand people will be killed, but the rest of the people will give God glory! An angel will sound a trumpet and the twenty-four elders seated on their thrones will worship God. God's temple in Heaven opens and the ark of His covenant is seen. Different types of storms and an earthquake will happen.

Open H†S Word

Chapter 12 Children of God are in a battle against the powers of this dark world and against the spiritual forces of evil in the heavenly realms. (Ephesians 6:12) If your heart is right with the Lord, know that He will protect you and has an escape route planned out. Nothing can harm you, but you have to trust and seek Him! Satan will try to do everything to have God's children give up on following Christ on the straight and narrow path.

Chapter 12 Satan's aim is to get and keep you away from Jesus Christ. Satan will use whatever it is to devour you and will lie to you. He will start as soon as you're born. The Father has given the Holy Spirit to His children whoever ask for the Holy Spirit. We are battling against evil forces in the heavenly realms. Satan and the evil spirits will attack you, but God is on your side. Seek God and continue to do so. Jesus has an escape route for you! But Satan will come back again and tempt you even harder. Seek God! Practice the power and the authority that Jesus has given you! Be victorious in Jesus Christ!

Chapter 13 The beast or the antichrist will rule the earth and will deceive people to make them think that he is God. The antichrist will perform great and miraculous signs. The people will worship the antichrist even though he is using proud words and blasphemies everything about God, such as God Himself, God's Name, dwelling place, and God's children in Heaven. If people don't worship the antichrist, death will be a threat.

Chapter 13 Satan will deceive people with two beasts and himself to make people worship them instead of Jesus. The beasts will perform signs, wonders, and speak not respectfully about God. Also the first beast will mock Jesus' Name, Jesus' dwelling place, and Jesus' children living in Heaven. A war will happen. Again Satan and the antichrist will deceive people; threaten people with death if people don't worship the beast or image that will be set up. The antichrist will force people to receive a mark on the forehead or on the right hand. Unless people have this mark, no buying or selling will take place.

Chapter 14 God's children will stand on Mount Zion with the Lamb who have His Name and His Father's Name written on their foreheads. This is incredible if you think about it!

Open H†S Word

Chapter 14 An angel will swing a sickle and the earth will be harvested. The people who blasphemy God will be thrown out of the city.

Chapter 14 The Lamb (Jesus) along with His 144,000 children with His and the Father's Name written on their foreheads will stand on Mount Zion. His children will sing a new song before the throne, the four living creatures, and the elders. The redeemed (people who believed and loved God with their whole heart) that don't cave under the pressures of this evil world will know the song. They follow Jesus wherever He goes. They walked the narrow path; led by the Holy Spirit. Three angels will proclaim worship God, drink the wine of adulteries, and drink God's cup of wrath to the earth. Rest will be no more because torment will fill the earth. The people who turn and believe in Jesus will be gathered up when angels sift through people when it's harvest time.

Chapter 15 When the seven last plagues are finished by the seven angels, God's wrath will be completed. Praises to God will be played and sung by the people who don't follow the antichrist. They will be called victorious! After unbelievers decide that they are done with living worldly, God gives them a new nature to live in. This may be what God is referring to in these verses, but don't take my word for it. I am just God's messenger.

Chapter 15 Seven angels will have the last of the seven plagues and as the result God's wrath will be completed. The people who overcome the beast, image, and his name will sing a song of praise with harps. In Heaven and in the temple the 10 Commandments is opened. The angels will wear what most people imagine angels' attire look like. Seven golden bowls will be handed out; filled with God's wrath. Smoke will fill the temple of the glory of God. With God's glory and power filling the temple, no one will enter in until the seven plagues are completed.

Chapter 16 Admirations will be spoken about God and to God. Evil spirits will stir up trouble once again. They will perform miraculous signs to deceive people.

Chapter 16 The seven angels will pour out the seven bowls of God's wrath on the earth. The bowl for the land will produce ugly and painful sores on the people who worship the beast and have his mark. The sea bowl will turn the water into blood making all living creatures die. The third bowl will make the rivers and springs of water turn into blood. The angel will sing about the Lord's judgments. The bowl for the sun will be given power to scorch people with fire. The intense heat will cause people to curse the name of God, refuse to repent, and glorify Him. The fifth bowl will plunge the beast's throne and kingdom into darkness. People will be in agony, but won't repent still. The sixth bowl will dry up the water of the great Euphrates. Evil spirits will come out again to deceive people. Jesus wants His children to stand firm in their faith of Him and to not grow weary of doing His will. Flashes of lighting, rumblings, peals of thunder, and a severe earthquake will be the final outcome of the seventh bowl. The city splits into three parts and the cities of nations will collapse. Hail falls on people and they will curse God.

Chapter 17 Many people make remarks about serious actions and events as if the actions and events are not something to be taken seriously. People will brush these actions and events off from their shoulders as if it's not a big deal. Abominations like prostitution and other commandments that God says not to do, will not be tolerated in the Last Days. If your name isn't written in the Book of Life, torture will come!

Chapter 18 God is a just God and Jesus will judge everyone according to how they lived their lives. The prostitution industry is booming in the world. Alcohol and drugs are drawing people. It's easy to get trapped in because these industries are around. Jesus will judge you according to how you live your life. Stand out for Jesus!

Chapter 19 Jesus will show up! He looks purer and Holy because He is! Think about His journey on earth. Who is He and how did He act around people in all sorts of circumstances? Think about His death. Faithful and True comes out on a white horse. Read Revelation 19:11-21 in the NIV to find out what happens next! Jesus is coming back!

Chapter 19 The great multitude in Heaven will shout praises to God. The twenty-four elders and the four living creatures will fall down, worship God, and sing praises to God. Jesus will come riding on a horse! Along with Jesus, will be His army. An angel will instruct the birds to gather God's children for the great supper

Open H†S Word

of God! The beast (antichrist) and his army will rage war again against Jesus and His army. The beast will be captured along with the false prophet and will be thrown into Hell. The rest of the army of the beast Jesus will kill by His sword of His mouth. All of the birds will eat the flesh.

Chapter 20 An angel will seize Satan and lock him up in the Abyss (bottomless pit) and sealed it over him, to keep him from deceiving the nations anymore until the thousand years were ended. After that, he must be set free for a short time. (Revelation 20:3) Remember in God's eyes a thousand years are a day. People will be judged.

Chapter 20 The dead, great and small, will be judge by Christ. Books and the Book of Life will be opened.

Chapter 20 An angel will seize Satan to bind him for a thousand years, which may be only for a day in God's eyes. Satan won't be able to deceive people until the thousand years are over. Souls will be in Heaven who are persecuted for their faith in Jesus and for the Word of God. Death has no power over you and you'll be reining with God the Father/Jesus for a thousand years as His priests.

Satan will be released to deceive the nations. Fire will come down from Heaven to devour Satan and his army. They will be thrown into Lake Of Fire where there's torment forever. Jesus will judge you by how you lived your life. Do you know with 100% without a doubt that your name is written in the Book of Life? Maybe you're not in the Book of Life so Hell might be your destination. Chapter 21 The Holy City, the New Jerusalem, will come down from Heaven to Earth dressed beautifully.

Chapter 21 God makes all things new! The Holy City, the New Jerusalem, the new Heaven, and the new earth will come into place. God will be with and live with His children face-to-face! He'll wipe away every tear! Christ is preparing Heaven, in which it'll be magnificent! The pearly gates and the streets of gold will be a couple of things that will be perfect. Beyond your imagination! Lord God Almighty and the Lamb will be the temple in the city. No sun or moon will be there because the glory of God will give light! Heaven is for those who have their name written in the Lamb's Book of Life!

Open H†S Word

Chapter 22 There's a river of the water of life flowing from the throne of God and of the Lamb. There's the tree of life on each side of the river bearing fruit each month. The leaves are for healing of the nations. Jesus' servants will serve Him! His children will see God, Jesus, and Holy Spirit face-to-face! No sun or moon will be there because the glory of God will give light! There won't be night. Jesus is coming soon! Jesus will reward everyone according to what they have done. Jesus is coming soon! Be ready! Listen to "All Who are Thirsty" by Kutless and "I Will Rise" by Chris Tomlin because the Holy Spirit has reminded me of these songs after reading this chapter.

End of <u>Revelation</u>

About The Author

Emily Zondlak is in love with Christ and in a relationship with Him! God is her number One in her life! God our Father has blessed Emily so much with family, friends, and experiences in her life that no words can express! She chooses to follow Him on His path for her life because His plan is far better than she could have done if she chose to do it on her own! Emily is determined to do everything as God lays the task down. Her Bible verse for her life is John 9:3. Many people think that handicapped people desire to live without their disability. This is not true for Emily! Her intimate relationship with God Almighty has molded her to be content in being physical disabled and nonverbal. Emily is on fire for the Lord Jesus Christ and wants to fragrance the world with Christ! Her anchor holds within the veil!

www.ingramcontent.com/pod-product-compliance
Lightning Source LLC
Chambersburg PA
CBHW072014110526
44592CB00012B/1301